JUST LET GO
Author: Victoria E. Kain
Graphic Illustrations by: | www.gritography.com
Layout Design by: Fycore Publishing
Development Editor: Jane Adams
Publisher: Fycore Publishing
www.fycore.com

This title is exclusively published by Fycore Publishing in over 190 Countries and available for purchase at Apple, Walmart, Sears, Barnes & Noble, Amazon, Sony, eBook Markets or wherever books are sold. If this title is not available at your favorite book retailer, please contact Fycore Publishing to assist you in ordering. Organizations with orders exceeding 500 copies may request a 90 day net invoice. No part of this book may be photocopied reproduced or transmitted in any form, to include digital, electronic without the express written permission from Fycore Publishing

International Standard Book Number:	9781619100282
International Digital eBook Number:	9781619100299
Library of Congress Control Number:	2016942945

Additional Formats May be Available for Pre-Order:

PHYSICAL			DIGITAL	
Trade Cloth	$29.95		CD/MP3 (Audio Book)	$17.95
Hard Back	$27.95		PDF Book	$14.95
Soft Back	$19.95		eBook	$9.99

For Inquiries or Additional Orders:

131 Sunset Ave Ste E#353
Suisun City CA, 94585
Office | (800) 470-FYCORE
Facsimile: | (800) 531-0190
Email: | publisher@fycore.com

Fycore Publishing
2016 © All Rights Reserved

JUST LET GO!

IT'S TIME TO CHANGE GEARS!

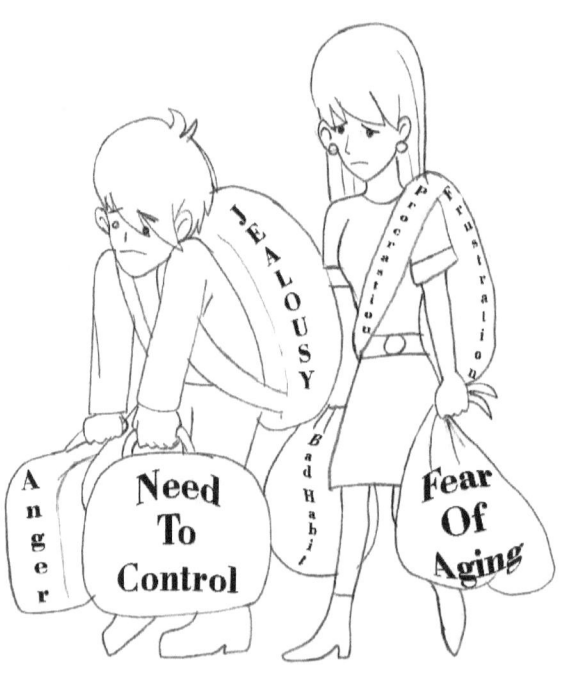

THIS BOOK WILL CHANGE YOUR LIFE FOREVER! NOW YOU CAN STOP DRAGGING NEGATIVE THOUGHTS, BEHAVIORS, AND ATTITUDES WITH YOU THROUGHOUT YOUR LIFE. DUMP THEM IN ONLY 7 DAYS BY DOING 5 SIMPLE THINGS!

Author Victoria E. Kain

Psychology Professor

JUST LET GO!

TABLE OF CONTENTS

Acknowledgments 4
Introduction DO IT NOW!..5
Power#1 Take Back Your Mental Power 8
Power #2 Identify and Control Your Positive and Negative Triggers........9
Power#3 Change Your Mind or It Will Change You 18
Power #4 Let Go of Negative Thinking..21
What is Mind Hoarding and Why is It Dangerous? 25
Power#5 Who Is the Boss of Your Brain.............................30
Remove Unnecessary Pressure..39
Men vs. Women on Carrying Excess Weight..............................44
Do You Want To Change? 51
Stop Allowing Things and People to Control You.......................53
Just Let Go of Superstitions...54
Just Let Go of Bad Habits...61
Just Let Go of Fear..64
Just Let Go of Anger/Frustration..70
Just Let Go of Jealousy..73
Just Let Go of Guilt...77
Just Let Go of Being a Victim..80
The "EVE" Effect...89
Tell Your Brain What You Want "It" To Believe....................92
Just Let Go of Procrastination..93
Just Let Go of Inhibitions..95
Just Let Go of the Need to Control..102
Why Should We Let Go of Negativity? 105
Just let go of the Fear of Aging...109
Epilogue 118
The Power of Positive Thinking..122

JUST LET GO!

ACKNOWLEDGEMENT

I want to thank all of my true friends and business associates who have openly expressed their positive thoughts regarding things that were heavy on their hearts as we've shared our dreams and goals with each other over the years.

Thank you Monarch, for being an open book for me to peer inside as I explored my own past and created pages to share with you and others. Barbara Jackson, much love to you for supporting me from all directions! We all experience life differently, but you bring all of your friends face to face with the reality of being "open" in sharing life and friendships. We are all on this journey called "life" and must fight to continue filling our hearts with the things we enjoy most.

Roma Obebe my dearest friend, I say to you, your kindness and unconditional support of my writing has been nothing short of phenomenal. My deepest gratitude goes to you for sharing your time and family with me. To my baby sister, Benita Byers, remember that in life, for a dream to come true you only have to wake up and get to work on making what you dreamed a "reality." Thank you all for your words of encouragement in this new journey! This is how I want to share my dreams with the world at large. Now, with pen and paper I can smile each day and call this "my work."

Thank you!

JUST LET GO!

Introduction

"DO IT NOW!"

Just Let GO

All humans, are instinctively prone to hold onto things they acquire in life. Whether it is people, bad thoughts, behaviors, attitudes or the like, we simply have a difficult time convincing ourselves to let go of anything we acquire, inherit or adopt even when it's in our best interest to do so. We struggle to accommodate the need to hold onto something even when our lives are at stake. Why do we do this? First, think about what controls our actions. That's right, "our brain!" It is approximately 3.03 lbs of wrinkly gray sponge looking matter that acts as the "boss" of our entire body. It is also aptly called the "executive center" because all of the directives and decisions we make come from "it"! Our brain controls just about everything we do, even when we are asleep! If you think for a moment…once again, using your brain, and consider the fact that our brain is controlling our functions and emotions. Walking, talking, swallowing, breathing, taste, smell…the brain controls it all. It does something even more serious though, relating to the subject of letting go. It stores and retrieves positive and "negative" memories.

In order to rid yourself of something "negative" you must first discover where the negative is coming from. Since the brain stores and retrieves data all day long, how does it do that? Well, it stores data when an event happens in our lives and then it retrieves it by using "triggers" which are many things around us that set off a request to the brain to dredge the memory of an event up. Let's look at an example of how that might work and see if this has happened to you. Let's use your Prom night. If you went to your high school prom, do you remember the dress or Tux you wore? Sure you do!

JUST LET GO!

It may be neatly tucked away in your closet until one day, as you are dressing, your eyes behold it! It majestically hangs there encapsulated with scores of memories waiting to be dredged up by your brain. Immediately your eyes send a signal to the brain to bring up "all" data related to the events surrounding the outfit. You begin thinking back to when you wore it. You picture the perfect fit on your "then" slender frame, which may not be so slender now, but still you remember that wonderful feeling. "Wow!" Your mind goes into a spin and you begin to reminisce about that evening long ago. You can almost hear the conversations, smell the night air and other special moments of that night. I guarantee you if you are reading this and you went to the prom, you might even look in your closet for your dress or tux to see if what is being said is true.

Well, we all know it is! That night was like no other and will be with you forever! Doesn't that positive memory feel good? Think about why you were able to remember so much about that event from just one glance at a faded too small outfit hanging in your closet. How could you possibly remember all of the details about that evening down to the smell of the flowers on your corsage? Yet, years later, here you stand still experiencing butterflies in the pit of your stomach which brings a smile to your face. Isn't that the good feeling you want to have more of in your life now? The simple answer is, "Yes!" You remember this night because it is a "positive" memory etched in your brain! Together, you and your brain decided to "keep" that amazing positive moment in your long term memory where all the good stuff is stored. Unfortunately, the brain does not discriminate.

It also holds "negative" memories and will dredge those up as well! But, every time you remember that Prom night or anything that brought you pleasure, a smile will appear on your face because you were "happy!" There are many things in life that make us "happy," yet happiness can be fleeting in these stressful times we live in. For this reason, we must learn how to harness positive thinking and not allow our brain to control everything we think and do. Our brain holds our memory and can go as far back as the "womb! That's right! Research shows that babies in the womb can remember hearing their mother's voices singing to them. That's the good news.

JUST LET GO!

However, the bad news is, by the same token, our trusty brains can "choose" to hold on to any "negative" memories or trauma we experience the same way it holds on to "positives." The difference is, the "negative" memories can cause a tremendous amount of pain in our lives that can cause other physical damage. That is why we must learn to let go of the negatives that may be controlling our thought patterns as quickly as possible so that we can experience more happiness. Remember that our brain believes it is in charge, but we must "re-train" ourselves to be in control of what our brain holds on to.

Think about it this way, the President of the United States is thought to be in complete control, yet he does not move until he gets approval from his cabinet members when "he" has to make decisions that will affect the country. We must learn how to talk to our brains and learn to accept the responsibility of making the final decision on what we should think and do. In time, we must accept that it is imperative that we begin steering our own course in life again or we could find ourselves brain deep in trauma that is difficult to escape! Each day, our brain works hard for us. If we tell our brain to pull up data, all we have to do is concentrate and it will happen. You know it will! What was the most recent big event in your life? Your brain is already responding!

This type of discussion helps us think about how we can easily overload our brains when we absorb too many negative thoughts at one time. More often, we forget the positive milestones we've accomplished in our lives as they are buried deeper each time we dredge up all the negative thoughts, actions and emotions we've encountered. Remember that our brain does what it does best, which is to store and retrieve both negative and positive data. Our goal is to be the "Boss" and tell our brain what to do with these thoughts. We will determine which thoughts we "keep, or the ones we dump!" We should work to stay mentally balanced when taking things in so we don't overload our system. Now that we are clear on who is in charge, your first challenge is to give your brain a "positive" assignment. "Go ahead…tell it what you want to do and see if it doesn't force you to start the process." Don't fight it and watch the 3.3 lb substance called "brain" actively work "for" and not "against" you to accomplish that goal! It's that simple!

JUST LET GO!

TAKE BACK YOUR MENTAL POWER
Power #1
"Take your brain off "AUTO PILOT" and take back the control you were designed to have over it"

As a driver is in control of an automobile and where it goes, humans should be in control of their brains and what it thinks and tells them to do. For many, that is not the case. For some, life takes over and causes us to put our brains on "auto pilot" and let it tell us what to do, when it should naturally be the other way around. We don't plan to do this, but events in our lives distract us and can cause us to lose focus and lack the energy needed to make some of the hard decisions we must make in life. Then, we simply let our brain "veg" and do whatever it wants to do for the moment and follow its commands like a slave. Over time, this creates a negative snowball effect in all areas of our lives.

When we allow our brain to make all the decisions without us, we may become despondent to things and people around us. Our finances may go astray, we may develop poor eating habits or don't exercise regularly. We may procrastinate getting things accomplished and the list can go on. When we see these things happening, we must recognize that we have put our brains on "auto pilot." In order to stop the madness of this process, we must take back our control and begin steering in the direction we want to go and not just end up somewhere wondering how you got there. Be determined to no longer allow "it" to tell "you" what to do and how to behave."

Now, you will learn how to be in control of everything you experience! When we recognize that we are consumed with negative thoughts, it is a true sign that our brain is actually controlling "us." *We have unknowingly switched* to mental "auto pilot" during some time, place or event in our lives. We may have done so unknowingly when we couldn't make the hard decision that faced us at the moment and we simply acquiesced to "whatever." It just seemed easier to just let things happen as they did.

JUST LET GO!

Our world today is filled with excessive violence, heartache, abuse, hatred and the like. It is no wonder our mind has become filled with negative data. With the evening news and work and taking care of our families, our lives have become clogged with negative thinking and simply is doing the best it can to survive. We do all we can to keep from snapping each day. Either way, it is now up to us to take back the control of our brain and control what we think and do. The first step is to agree that we should take our brains off auto pilot and begin examining the reason we are collecting and holding onto too many negative thoughts. Next, we must understand what causes the negatives to manifest themselves within us and find ways to head them off the same as a migraine sufferer heads off the migraine by recognizing and reacting to the *"aura"* before the pain begins. Let's attack this invisible foe head on!

Power #2 Identify *and Control Positive and negative* Triggers

Let's discuss our invisible foe, *"negative triggers"* that we have learned to obey so eagerly. First, what is a "trigger? Depending on how this word is used, it could be described in many ways. *A small device that releases a spring or catch and sets off a mechanism for firing a gun. Or, in the instance of the brain; an event or circumstance that "acts" as that mechanism and is the cause of a particular action, process or situation.* In short, a mind trigger could be anything that causes a reaction to recall something from our past that creates pain or pleasure. Triggers may cause us to dredge up negative feelings which is always followed by negative behavior. We know there are different reactions to negative triggers so let's look at an example of how this could look. You may be watching a movie with your new love and the movie depicts a jilted party in the relationship. You become emotional and begin to cry when you see the woman or man begging their partner not to leave them.

JUST LET GO!

Your eyes picked up the signal of pain from the movie you watched which sent a signal to your brain to create the emotion for tears which in turn told your brain that you were feeling pain. Once again, the "trigger" has gone into action and engaged your brain to respond by dredging up only hurt feelings from the past to identify with what you are seeing on T.V. You don't realize it, but you begin feeling the pain "you" felt when you had "your" break up with an old flame or a good friend jilted you. You remember that it felt the same way as this character is portraying their pain in the movie. Now, the 'trigger" causes you to take your emotions to another level. You begin to *behave* in line with the trigger. Unfortunately, your new love sitting next to you has no idea what just happened in your brain. Then a battle of wits begin to engage to accommodate the trigger: Here's how it might sound:

"Is there something wrong? " He or she might ask.

"No!" you respond, in a sullen manner.

"Well why are you looking so down?" They might ask.

"Did I do something wrong?" And here it comes…

"ALL MEN ARE DOGS!!!" you might state, and the war begins. This scenario could go for either gender. The "trigger" and the brain have worked hand in hand and set the situation off. It has done its job and no one gets any sleep that night. "Negative" memories, unlike "positive" ones seem to stick with us longer also.

Millions of people experience this scenario and have no clue why. They simply accept it and if it doesn't go too far, they make up and move on. For many reasons we hold onto negative thoughts, behaviors, and even relationships longer than we should. Why do we do this and "sabotage" opportunities for more positive memories? We don't know, we just do! We quickly forget how far we've come to be able to "see" the light at the end of the tunnel and then run head first into the oncoming train of life. Soon we may even become afraid of knowing how to accept feeling "good" about something because we have not felt "good" in such a long time. Eventually, if unchecked, we could teach ourselves to accept pain and misery as our only option. True, it is not easy to let go of negative feelings.

JUST LET GO!

But it is truly not impossible either! You only have to "want" to be more positive and train yourself to react differently towards the good effects that positive thinking and behaving brings you. When something positive happens in our lives, we enjoy the moment and instinctively want to look for the "next" positive so we don't think much about it. The brain tucks it away neatly. But negatives seem to be more plentiful and are things you "don't" want to repeat so the brain seems to react faster to the triggers we encounter. The more negative triggers the more negative feelings and behavior. How can we halt the chain reaction and avoid repeating a negative action? We must now replace these negatives with positives and train our brain to think differently!

EMBRACE POSITIVE TRIGGERS

Simply put; an emotional *trigger* is the mechanism that engages the brain to believe that someone has taken or plans to take something of value away from you. When this trigger happens, it causes the brain to dredge up all data associated with an event, person, place or thought and then you "react" to it. You might react with anger, fear or even frustration. But in order to control this, you must learn how to quickly rationalize your behavior so what you do will make sense. The key here is to recognize when an emotional "trigger" is taking place and then you can immediately address it on the spot. Doing so, tells the brain that you "know" what is happening and it does not have to send any further signals to the body to respond unnecessarily. Sort of the same way a panic attack is approached. It is a "fight or flight" indication, but the body is not actually being harmed. But, if the brain "thinks" it is in danger, it gears up to defend...NOTHING! You can tell yourself that you are not in harm's way and if you "choose" to believe it, you can have the potential panic episode halted on the spot! Guaranteed! The choice will be yours, but first, you must practice this routine because the brain is smart enough to know when you "don't" believe something and will quickly override the thought without your permission. Let's see what this might look like in real life.

JUST LET GO!

A true scenario - *A woman was sitting at her desk at work and all of a sudden her body began swaying in her chair and she felt as if she was falling. She immediately grabbed hold of the arm of the chair to stop the fall, but she was still firmly planted in the chair. Now frightened, her brain went into action to figure out what had happened. It began trying to figure out what had caused her to feel this way. She occasionally suffered from headaches but had not had one and wasn't sure if that was what had just happened. She soon dismissed it but the thought of the reaction from her body feeling as if it was falling never left her mind.*

She went home and told her husband about it and with no answers still she went to bed. Several days later the episode happened again when she least expected it. It frightened her even more this time because now there had been several episodes of this issue of dizziness and the feeling of falling even when seated. The next time it happened, she began to sweat profusely, her breathing became labored and she felt that her digestive tract was becoming out of control. She knew she was dying and had no choice but to seek medical help.

She went to doctor after doctor. Weeks later after brain scans, blood tests and wearing medical devices to see if she was having seizures, nothing was found to stop the painful issue of her dizziness and now shortness of breath and other out of control body issues. Finally after several months it was being suggested that it was all in her "HEAD." She decided to see a different doctor who examined her and had her lay on the examining table. The doctor took hold of the woman's head and told her she would move it from one side to the other. When she did, the woman shrieked "Woah, I just got very dizzy!" The doctor immediately stated, "I believe you have "vertigo." The doctor gave the woman a prescription and told her to take it and it should relieve her symptoms.

JUST LET GO!

She also told the woman that with the vertigo, when the woman would become dizzy and unsteady she would go into a "panic attack" which caused the other symptoms of feeling the uncontrolled body functions, shortness of breath and the feeling that she was dying. The woman went home extremely happy and took the tablet as mentioned. She made some changes to her water intake and from that day forward, she has not had the issue of the dizziness again as such. The point in this scenario is this. The woman initially had an issue. The brain determined that something was drastically wrong. Because she didn't know what it was, when this issue would happen, the woman would go into the "fight or flight" mode of a panic attack which caused the feeling of imminent death!

Now that the woman had a "name" for her condition, she knew that it was NOT an imminent death issue. If she felt small dizziness before the medications kicked in, she no longer panicked. She would tell her brain, "It is effects of vertigo." I am okay! From that, the brain sends no panic signals to the body to protect her from danger. Remember, when the brain has no answers, it begins to do all sorts of things because it is being flooded with requests from us as to what is wrong. We must remember to stay calm and make sure that we are in as much control as we can be when faced with unexpected issues. Does the woman remember the event? Sure, but it no longer cripples her thought process. She has shut down the brain on that issue unless something else comes up to be added to this matter.

Memories are like this. Whatever the event, the brain will hold on to that memory for as long as we choose to keep it. The brain will only bring that event up if we experience a trigger. The trigger could be; seeing the way someone combed their hair, brushed their teeth, chewed their food, a word spoken or the way someone walked. Even our sense of smell could come into play when we detect a certain aroma in the air. All of these external factors can trigger emotions to manifest things in our brains. We may see someone do something that triggers a certain feeling in us and the list can go on.

JUST LET GO!

Our five senses act as accomplices to many of our triggers. Remember the account we just mentioned in the beginning of the book about the high school prom dress/tux you saw in your closet? You may not have thought about this outfit until you were dressing in your closet and your "*eyes*" focused on it which became the "trigger" point. The garment represented a happy moment in time. Your brain used the outfit as the focal point for that timeline to trigger your memories of that evening.

Once your eyes beheld the object, the mental image caused a trigger and your brain caused you to feel happy and it instinctively pulled up all the data in its long term storage surrounding that day. That was a positive "trigger." It contributed to your happiness in that moment! Positive triggers can make you feel awesome! When you feel good, you can do many things and are not as inhibited. Consider also that positive memories fade quickly. We are always looking for that next good moment to top the last one. If you watch some animals, they only seem to remember the "good" things first and the bad if it is repeated. Once you've had your moment of positive Déjà vu you move on. It's unnatural to stay in Déjà vu mode forever. Your brain simply shuts down the trigger effect and it closes up shop relating to the positive memory and you focus on something else.

You will not go through the day with the prom dress or Tux draped around your shoulders to remember the event. You simply cherish the good memories you had and create ways to make new "positive" ones. You may call an old friend to rekindle the sparks if you are able to do so. But your current life soon takes over and when your brain no longer needs those triggers you simply make room in your closet one day and toss out the faded prom dress or suit. However, that memory will only come up when you sit down and "choose" to think about that night. This means "you" are in full control of your thoughts and what you dredge up. This is where you want to be in all of your thought processes. You want to be in control of when "you" choose to think about something as opposed to your "brain" dredging it up because of a "trigger."

JUST LET GO!

DON'T LET NEGATIVITY BE YOUR NEW CHAOS

Let's look at this a little further. We're discussing negative thinking a bit longer only to examine how it comes in and how we may choose to hold on to it longer than we should. Sometimes, negativity can become our comfortable chaos when we allow it to become our new bedfellow. What this means is that some people hold on to negatives because they have grown accustomed to doing so. This old companion "misery" is neatly tucked in their lives and gets to reside with them until their own demise. If we are not careful, over time, we may become complacent with misery because of the fear of facing "happiness." It sounds strange to hear that some people may choose to hold on to a doom and gloom situations, but it's true!

We all know what they say, "misery loves company." For some, pity may even get them a bit of attention, but even that is fleeting, so they continue to manufacture doom and gloom. Have you ever known two negative people who compete for the same attention, this is what you might hear…

"I broke my leg and it took me forever to heal." The other person might say, "I broke my arm and my family had to hand feed me for months. Another may say…"My dog died right after I delivered their 10 pups and I had to hand feed each of them every day. The other, trying to get that last piece of sympathy, "Well, I had six operations all in one year and had to leave my job…woe is me…"

There are many people who do the "one ups" on how bad their lives are and seem to love it. That is because their lives are not really that bad, they just need more attention. They have learned how to manufacture what they need but they really are still in some measure of control of their thinking. Let's face it. No one is blissfully happy 24/7.

JUST LET GO!

But for the masses, most people want to be happy! Still, many may feel that the constant for them is "unhappiness." Even when happiness "does" come around, these individuals don't believe it will last long so they soon drift back into the "unhappy" state of mind which feels more like normal to them. It sounds a little strange but think about it for a moment. In the face of "misery" feeling "happy," becomes a new "fear." Some are afraid to be too happy believing it will be short lived. Some even wonder why they should bother with the temporary enjoyment of happiness. They think it's a waste of time to seize the moment and cherish it! For these type of people, when you say something positive, they will give you its "negative" equal.

They do this because happiness for them is naturally a "fleeting" emotion. They focus too much on the ultimate ebbing away by old age and death and become obsessed with the "end" which hasn't happened yet. We should "choose" to dwell on the positives in the midst of all negative situations. We can choose to adopt positive thinking as a way of life and refute negativity altogether. That doesn't mean that in the face of a dire situation we are blissful.

It only means that we realize that becoming morbidly fearful over a matter to the point that we can't function, is going over the edge! We must stay balanced. It is a sad truth that many people may experience a deep pain from ruminating over negative life events. But what does this solve? Many just like you are burdened with hoarding negative mental baggage. They constantly dredge up garbage memories, bad relationships, pain and suffering from abuses and even hand down superstitious beliefs from their forefathers and mothers that they never even understood! This seems to be the soup of the day in our 21st century to carry old "stuff" around of no value. The more complex our lives, the more toxic our minds become. Some experts even say that "we are what we eat." If that is true, then consuming garbage thoughts will beget garbage thinking and behaving. They say that even changing our physical diets can help our mental wellbeing! Aren't you sick and tired of being sick and tired? It's time to do something about it once and for all! Now this is getting serious!

JUST LET GO!

Whether we want to or not, we all hold onto things from our past. The loss of a loved one can take us into a mental and physical vortex. Going through a divorce can cripple us mentally and destroy our self-worth and self-esteem. Single parents may ruminate over the "what if's" of the lost relationship with the father of their children who they loved dearly. Illness can ravage our existence causing a break down in our mental barriers which spills into our families lives too. However, this happens more often when we readily digest toxic mental waste! At some point, we may feel worthless and accept that feeling that way is our new "Normal." This world has lost many beautiful people all because of their inability to JUST LET GO of the very things that contributed to taking them out…Negative thinking! Let's examine more reasons why we should dump this toxic thinking. This book is not a cure all, but will help reset your mental circuits and rid you of the bad habits you've grown accustomed to repeating. Now you will choose to develop positive habits in only 7 days and become a happier "YOU!" So what do you do? It's simple! You start by turning the page.

Meet Happy!

JUST LET GO!

"Change Your Mind or It Will Change You!
Power #3

Just Let GO

With the thought of misery and unhappiness engulfing our lives minute by minute, we all must learn how to change our minds from "negative" to "positive thinking quickly! How do we do it? First, you must identify your own negative thought patterns, behaviors and triggers. Once you are clearly aware of what negatives you dwell on and understand why, you can begin to change the way you think and eliminate the triggers associated with the thoughts. When you analyze how mental negativity impacts the whole body and ultimately your happiness, you will be able to look back on your life and identify how and why things may have taken a turn for the worse in your life or at least why you feel so bad about things.

Consider this. For some, it is noted that there is a certain uncanny "comfort" in carrying around the very toxic baggage that makes them miserable. Negative thoughts may arise when we feel bad about something. Or when we are ill or hurting emotionally and understand that some issues in life are out of our control. But remember that once we open the box of "negatives" our brain is geared to dredge up everything possible to keep us in that negative state. Simply put, it's the brains job to store and retrieve data! However, when we set our brains on "negative" auto pilot, it can work 24/7. Unchecked, this could put us in a catatonic mindset enabling us to function normally. What most of us don't understand or focus on, is that "we" can tell our BRAIN what to do!!! That's right!

JUST LET GO!

We understand that some things are difficult to let go of in life when we have been traumatized. In those instances, people are encouraged to seek professional help first. This is the best advice in those instances where there may be something deep seated that you need assistance to cope with. A professional can help you deal with the emotional aspects of letting go of things that are subliminally entrenched. It takes time to remove or minimize deep trauma and must be handled professionally! But, if the concerns are more superficial, you can work through them by telling your brain a few simple things to keep it from going to "auto pilot."

Many people may not seek to change their current mindset due to pain, guilt or shame of an event or circumstance. Some may simply be too tired to tackle making another change in their lives. They may try to live with the event in silence only to be attacked by it with trigger after trigger until the negatives surface in an out of control emotion or behavior. At that point, we become hardwired for negative responses and life becomes a roller coaster of let downs unless you can find your way off the vicious cycle of toxic mind waste that the brain dumps out daily. Some people ask...

But...how can I change from negative to positive thinking?

In order to heal and change from negative to positive thinking, you must first learn to halt the triggers and the mental regurgitation of the negative information your mind is force feeding you daily. You will learn how "not" to re-ingest negatives. There are many ways negative thinking can cripple our lives. It can do more damage than we realize. *First* it can cause anger, fear or physical reactions such as headaches then depression, insomnia and panic attacks. *Second*, if not checked, it may go into heart palpitations, mood swings, infertility, back aches, or poor immune system response which is much more serious!

JUST LET GO!

With all these physical symptoms that may be directly related to prolonged negative thinking and behavior, it is imperative that we find ways to relieve ourselves of the culprit that is taking over our lives. The easiest way to begin taking our life back is by taking one step at a time and first acknowledging that there is an issue. Once the acknowledgement is accepted, you will begin changing your brain's way of looking at the negatives you encounter in life. You will do this one day at a time for 7 days. Now it is time to sit down or stand up and have a heart to head talk with yourself and say…"NO MORE!" It is time to take back "ALL" of the power you have given your brain in the past!

You will teach your brain to stop dredging up negative data to past the time away when you have nothing else to do or you are feeling down because you may not feel happy at the moment. Instead of thinking negative thoughts, pick up a book and read a good story. Reading excites the imagination and creates memorable thoughts to store in your brain. For every "positive" new memory you create, discard two negative memories. You will tell your brain to "Stop" wasting away your beautiful life on old traditions and superstitious thinking that keeps you in a negative state of mind that does not work for you today in the 21st century! You will strive to make new traditions for yourself and your family. You can conquer not looking back at your negative past as if it was your shadow. Now is the time to collect the pieces of our puzzled lives and reconnect those pieces in order to never be reminded of how badly they were broken in the past.

It's time to "stop" re-infecting ourselves with the same toxic negative thinking that we use to bind the very wounds we seek to heal! Is it practical to think that we can heal ourselves using the same things that infect us??? No!!! The wound here is negative speech, negative thoughts and negative behavior. We must systematically interject into our minds and hearts "positive" thoughts, attitudes and actions and make application of those if we are to heal.

JUST LET GO!

We must "not" allow our minds to dwell in the dark places of our past which only rob us of ever having any resemblance of a positive future. The motivational aspects of this book and others in this collection will help you focus on how and why you must **"Just Let Go"** of negative baggage that takes the joy out of living a fruitful life. Have you recently found yourself putting on extra pounds, losing hair, biting nails, stuttering, unexplained depression, drinking, smoking, high blood pressure, unwarranted criticising of others that are successful, jealousies, resentment or exhibiting obsessive compulsive behaviors in any fashion and can't figure out why??? If so, it is time to change your mind because it is changing you!!! How do you change it?

LET GO OF NEGATIVE THINKING

Be careful what you say, because your brain is listening!
Power #4

 Just Let GO

That statement above is very true and becomes very powerful when we keep it in the forefront of our minds when speaking. You've heard of speaking your mind. Well, our brain is alive and active. It is the executive center of our body and is very powerful so don't abuse, misuse or refuse to acknowledge the respect we must give this organ that controls our very lives with our help. In the medical field, if the brain is dead, the body is considered dead even if the heart is still beating. We must be careful what we tell ourselves because it's your brains job to actually do what "YOU" tell it to do!" So in essence, when you speak, your brain listens and carries out your wishes. Sort of like a Genie in a bottle!

JUST LET GO!

Be careful what you think, even in a fleeting moment, because the brain has captured that thought and is sprinting through the archive of events from your past to select just the right juicy "trigger" to bring face to face with the thought you just had. Once the trigger is selected, the brain pairs the new thought with an old memory and now you are face to face with lights, cameras, "ACTION!" If you tell yourself nothing about this trigger you have just encountered, you have inadvertently put your brain on "auto pilot" and it makes an "executive decision" and moves forward without you! Depending on what you are thinking, coupled with our trusty trigger the brain has aptly provided, you may be prone to crying, rage, anger, frustration, swearing, taking a drink you didn't want to take or other things.

If you want your brain to stop dredging up negative images, data and memories, simply tell it to "STOP!!!" Remember, it's listening! Be specific about what you DON"T want your brain to do because as they say…"It has a mind of its own." Of all the powers that we do have, realizing that our brain is literally at our disposal is usually the furthest thing from our minds. If you have ever watched a new born or toddler, they try to do everything on their own because they have a what? "Brain!" No one has to tell them to do what they do but parents keep them safe by telling them when to stop…knowing their limitations. For adults, we hesitate doing things because we may have experienced failure in certain areas of life.

Letting go of anything that causes distress in our lives is a function we must practice for survival in this anxiety riddled society. When toxic negative thoughts become the mainstay for human existence, we swiftly become morbidly toxic in our thinking from the time we get out of bed in the morning until we lie down at night. Because of the negative conditions we face, nutritionists, scientist and the trusty internet give scores of urgent messages on ways to DETOX, DETOX and more DETOX for our bodies, yet, we don't hear as much about "detoxing" our minds which is the core of many of our physical ailments!

JUST LET GO!

They say that the only way we can survive the toxic foods, water, and air we breathe daily, is to rid ourselves of as much toxicity that we can to protect ourselves. So, what do we do? We buy organic foods which is supposed to give us less pesticides. We filter our water to make it more "alkaline." We use air purification systems in our homes and vehicles to filter out some of the bacteria and allergens in our air. However, with all the positive ways we are told we can stay healthy physically, we give little thought to keeping a healthy "mind." We have heard that many patients with life threatening illnesses such as "cancer" do well when they go into special medical facilities because the physical disease is not the only thing being treated.

These centers care for the "whole" person!" They recognize that the "mind" is what "feeds" the body, and it is at the root of what is happening to either speed up or slow down the healing process from within! When we ingest toxic mental negativity in the form of illness, tragedy, trauma, mental, physical and psychological abuses, it in turn produces "stress, anxiety, depression, insomnia, thoughts of suicide, and other ills within us. Our mind will naturally gravitate towards all the "negative" data it can dredge up. Our body doesn't stand a snowballs chance in a thousand degree furnace if we do not get to the root cause of what really troubles us. We must remove negativity from our lives as a main staple. Our brains are literally becoming a human "waste dump" for everything we ingest mentally and physically!

CAN I ELIMINATE NEGATIVE THINKING?

Yes! But, here's the catch. The only way we can have a miniscule chance for survival in this negatively charged world, is to find ways to detoxify not only our bodies from the poisons in our food, water and air, but we must simultaneously rid our "minds" of toxic mental sludge from abuses that clog our synapses and bury our creativity and happiness! Have you ever considered the News you watch?

JUST LET GO!

What about the internet? Everyone who is up to date, is on the internet for something or other. The world at large is teaching our children to become "tech" savvy and inundating children from K-12 to use all of the technology available. By the time our next generations are on the scene, most of them will have destroyed their retinas from blearing for countless hours into a computer screen, iPad, iPod, iPhone, tablet or the like. They will have arthritis from using their "thumbs" to navigate the endless games and texting to amuse themselves! Now is the time to consider drastically "reducing" the amount of time you and your loved ones "surf" the internet and drown in reality shows. If not halted, you will soon find yourself "drifting" out to sea to a negative mind hoarding island.

We must act swiftly to remove negative mental baggage as it surfaces in our thoughts, through the triggers we encounter! Change your mental environment and it will change your mental outlook! When mental toxins begin to manifest themselves in our daily lives, they do so in many forms. Negative outbursts, nighttime arguments, a lack of creativity, impatience, procrastination, jealousy, fear, unexplained anxiety, fits of anger, guilt syndrome, unknown weight gain or loss, alcohol or drug use and other habits we see exhibited by people today. We have seen firsthand, many celebrities who have succumbed to overuse of drugs and alcohol, in order to "wind down" or cope from the constant mental high of having to smile and perform for the infamous "camera."

The mental strain and the lack of an ability to rid themselves of the constant barrage of requests to perform, ultimately takes over. While the lives of those seem glamorous on the outside, when the general public is able to peer into the lives of those after their demise, it is a shocking truth of how their lives mimic ours and are fragile to say the least. Their troubled brains were served with a constant state of false happiness which was chased with loneliness and unhappiness. As mentioned earlier, it is not normal to be happy 24/7 or to be in the blissful Déjà vu mode all day. There has to be a balance!

JUST LET GO!

This may be why more of the younger celebrities are trying to be more of themselves because they recognize the dangers that exist in the realm of stardom. Negative thinking doesn't just appear on its own. This way of thinking is learned and becomes entrenched throughout life. We become inundated with negative issues that drive our mental capacity to the brink! When we are at the brink, our physical bodies begin to shut down. When all these areas become excessive, our brain hoards all the negative data it has collected over our lifetime and we begin "ruminating" over various negative things which worsens the issues we must naturally face. Then this begets "Mind hoarding."

"What is Mind Hoarding? Why is it Dangerous?"

Mind hoarding is a nasty process whereby the brain becomes imbalanced and holds onto every piece of negative data it encounters in your life that can be stored. It's the same mindset as a person who hoards "things." Their dwellings can become filled to the brim with "stuff," that they do not need, want or will ever use. Their brains have convinced them that these "things" have a purpose in their lives and even though some of the things do, the imbalance comes in because they can't see where the hundreds of other things are not being utilized at all, yet they continue to collect them. In this instance a "mind" hoarder uses their "brain" as the "house," they fill with negative thoughts, attitudes, perceptions and behaviors. This can create many negative personality traits in people along with psychological issues, acute anxiety and depression.

JUST LET GO!

When the mind is hoarded, it is so full of negative data, that if not dumped, it will spew out negative speech or behavior on its own. These negative actions are usually repeated, whether real or imagined. The mind hoarder continues to fill their brain cells up the same way a hoarder of "things" fill up their homes or other dwellings. All for the sake of satisfying an untouchable need to take control of something in their lives in the present or from their past. Over time, their brain becomes "comfortable" with the negatives it has acquired and believes it "needs" them. Soon these mental things bring them a false sense of comfort. Some may crowd their minds to keep from thinking about something painful. Some may want to forget an attack they encountered. Being surrounded by "physical" things could give a sense of protection from their past or future attackers in life. With this thought, the brain will never let go of anything negative it encounters. Soon it will have its owner act out scenarios like a rehearsed Broadway play. Mind hoarding can be dangerous because of the negative effects it can have on your entire life!

It is this invisible culprit "mind hoarding" that plagues most humans when there is not enough "positives" in their memory banks to draw from to combat the negative feeds they are hit with daily. If we do not counteract this collection of negative data and "discard" some of it daily by interjecting positives, over time this capsulized entity "mind hoarding" fills up like a flu virus cell and when it bursts, it causes a replication of its negative self-encompassing thoughts, attitudes and behaviors.

If left unchecked, we can become "infected" with the negative mindsets and easily succumb to depression, stress, PTSD and other issues that could cause us to "ruminate" over things creating a chain reaction of distresses. Though the mental and physical pain is real, when the mind continues to recreate its own "trauma," by "ruminating," positive thinking can be buried. The mind then must be "unlocked" in order to fuel itself with any positives you may experience in the future. If not, our brain will become overloaded and become unable to recognize or respond to anything positive over time.

JUST LET GO!

There has to be a starting point on letting go of "anything" negative in life. Start now! Once we can rid ourselves of the tendency to "mind hoard," we can ultimately beat the ugly habit of harboring negativity and gain a positive outlook. This in turn helps us conquer other issues such as fear, anger, procrastination, jealousy, guilt, anxiety, resentment, fear of aging, over eating, over drinking, internal victimization, inhibitions, the need to control others and more. Remember, most of the *behaviors we have,* are learned over the course of many years through a life process cycle called "***classical conditioning.***" This book is not a cure-all, but a wake-up call addressing areas of life where we may create, hold on to and replay negative thoughts over and over in our brains which inadvertently restrict our positive thinking ability.

Sometimes, we create negatives in our lives for the purpose of filling a void. We may get into a "go nowhere" relationship where you are clear from the beginning, there is no future in it for us. We allow ourselves to bask in the superficial comfort of feeling that the person is there for us. You may be trying to make yourself feel better about a previous situation that ended badly so you drag those hurt feelings and latch on to someone else to try and mask the previous failed relationship by trying to make the "round" peg fit in the "square" hole. No matter how hard you try, it will never fit. Your brain knows it and it keeps the negative data lurking in the background until something "triggers" your brain to get real about the matter.

Sometimes in these types of relationships, you may wonder why you gain or lose excessive amounts of weight or have that heavy feeling in your stomach when you see that you are not completely connected to the person you are with. When you get that feeling, it is your brain reminding you of why you are there in the first place. You have settled for something that you really didn't want, but you have accepted that it was the best you could do at the time and to save face from your previous situation. Your brain may even cause you to have guilt feelings that are negative.

JUST LET GO!

So you bite the bullet and pretend it is right for you but your brain knows better. It will remind you often of what you really don't have in the long run. It's like being fed with an empty spoon. You are never completely nourished and eventually, you starve to death emotionally. Most people have never considered why they choose this way of life, but now is the time to "THINK!" For most of us, when we read something that jars our memory towards an *issue* we face, we tend to focus on it in order to resolve it if it's important to us…if not, we just let it lay there until a "trigger" causes us to react.

If our brain is not clear, it simply packs away the negative feelings in its mental suitcase and we carry the unfinished issue around until something else "jars" our memory again to resolve an unresolved issue. This process begets "procrastination," a process by which you "put off" things you should complete but don't, because of mental or physical fatigue. If for no other reason, this book will "*jar*" our minds to address some areas of concern so you can live a less stressful "EVERY DAY!" Think about this; anything that weighs us down, we naturally try to accommodate the extra weight. If its physical weight gain, we buy larger clothing to make us feel comfortable in the body we are in.

If it is mental weight, we make room in our day to **ruminate** over things in our already crowded minds. Those things that bother us, we respond to all the "***triggers***" that keep the negative mental entity alive inside our head. Instinctively, because we may not be able to resolve an issue at the moment, we try to hold on to the negative thought, reasoning that we will go back to it at a later time not realizing that these are the unfinished things that "crowd" our minds leaving our brain filled with things waiting to be resolved. With no resolution, at inopportune times, that same "negative" might appear in the form of stress, negative behavior and the like, depending on what it is.

JUST LET GO!

We might begin blaming ourselves for not being able to accomplish anything because of other unfinished business our brain reminds us of. We think we don't have time to complete this business, but we do! Then, when we are not hired for a job we wanted, we add that to our unfinished things or failures in our minds instead of chalking it up to the better candidate was selected for the job and move on. In all reality, one thing had nothing to do with the other. However, our brain convinces us that if we didn't resolve a matter or accomplish a specific task, it then punishes us with negative thoughts and the list will grow after each unsuccessful opportunity we encounter.

Over a lifetime, our brains become a mental dumping ground for unresolved issues. This unrelenting internal "to do" list that we will never get to will be ever present. Did you know that humans are born with 1.1 trillion brain cells at birth? We lose 10,000 brain cells per day which is a drop in the bucket, but why waste the brain cells on harboring negative thoughts. Utilize those cells for more positive things and let the brain do what it does best. Who thinks about this? Most of us don't! Our brain does its job and "STORES" data we've collected along with all the 10 second thoughts we have, including the one about us not cleaning out our closet that we didn't want to tackle! But why do we process data this way? Well, the simple answer is, your brain is like this: when you think of something, it records the thought in your long or short term memory. Either way, it is in your brain for keeps until you do something with the data or a "trigger" dredges it up for further action. If you decided you should clean your closet and spoke those words, remember, your "brain" is listening to what you say to yourself and to other people.

For that reason, be careful what you say, do and think because it will simply go to work to figure out a way to get the job done to your satisfaction whether it's right or wrong, with or without your assistance. In order to take control of this process, let's unveil the secret to harnessing the power to stop the mental madness of negative thinking and see how we can gain control of "all" the "unfinished" business in our heads.

JUST LET GO!

"Who Is The Boss of Your Brain?"

Power #5 *"Take Control of Your Brain!!!"*

Just Let GO

Remember that from birth, you have been in control of your brain. The 1.1 trillion brain cells you acquired were designated to "YOU!" You may have been too young to know it at the time, but it was there helping you learn what you learned as you grew up. You learned how to speak, walk, run, and everything else along with learning to manipulate things and people to get anything you wanted. Knowing that we have been in control of our brain from the beginning really should tell us something. The brain is taking its commands from you whether you know it, like it or not. If you think of something by speaking to yourself internally or otherwise, your brain is picking up those signals and will decide what to do with it.

However, it is "YOU" who should actually make the final decision! Don't take this action of controlling your brain lightly because it is a serious matter even for the smallest things we tell it to do. When we take control of "how we think and what we think about" we can then adjust the outcome of that thought to the extent of our control of the situation. When you tell yourself that you must do something, the brain captures the command. However, if you never get it done, every time you repeat that command, the brain moves past it because nothing has changed about what you have said you wanted to do originally. If you do not move towards adding a new element to the command to get the task done, the brain puts it on hold. This then becomes "procrastination." At some point, you must "add" an action word to the original command that takes it to the next level in the brain to do something about it.

JUST LET GO!

Let's review how this might look and show you how you can "Change your mind." This is one way to stop your brain from piling up data in your mental data bank and overdrawing your mental account. You pay high penalties each time you mentally overdraw your brain. Once you are able to master this process you will acquire a positive balance in your mental bank to draw positive thoughts from. Here's how it works!

"How Does Your Brain Respond to Commands?"

If you say you are going to clean your closet and do not "clean it," the thought is tucked away in your brain on its' "to do" list until something "jars" your memory...i.e. tripping over a shoe in the closet while picking out something to wear. You acknowledge the mess in the closet but haven't done anything about it. Then your brain reminds you of what you said, "I'm going to clean the closet."

Funny thing is, the brain remembers that you said those words before and didn't do anything about it. It knows you already have that thought stored so it keeps it on the "to do" list...just like it is. Nothing will happen with that task in your head now until you add one new component or action to that original statement in your brain.

The brain is cleverly aware that you said "I am going to clean my closet" but you didn't go back in the closet to clean it. You simply pulled the cotton dress out and went on your way. But you gave your brain a command in reference to what you "wanted" to do but since you didn't do it, you think you don't have time, but you do! In order to remove this thought from your mental "to do" list, you must add one more element or command to your original statement to set it in motion to be accomplished.

You will say this...

JUST LET GO!

"I am going to clean my closet "TODAY!"

Now, the brain recognizes that **TODAY** added to "I am going to clean my closet," becomes a new command and it senses an urgency and begins to look for ways to clear your mental and physical schedule so you can resolve the issue of cleaning your closet! It will even dredge up the memory of you "tripping" over the shoes that were out of place because the closet needed cleaning.

Once you set this task in motion and clean the closet, the thought of cleaning your closet miraculously "DISAPPEARS" from the brains "to do" list and you don't think about cleaning your closet anymore! You do, however smile when you walk in the neatly organized closet and this too is registered in the brain as a great accomplishment! The brain has no reason to keep that original command of cleaning your closet in its memory anymore! Believe it or not, you can do this with ANY thought you have in your brain! That's right! It can be done right now! Think about something you want to get done and you know you can do it. You only need to "Change your mind" and add a new value to original commands and set things in motion to get the job done! Procrastination can be cured this way as well!

Now you can begin reading Novels as a way to relax each day. Take 30 minutes out of your schedule to put away the negative thoughts you've accumulated and delve into a good book. You might begin to read to your child each night before bed, or go back to school to complete your college degree, or even lose a few unwanted pounds. You may decide to change jobs, or your hairdo or even clean up an outdated credit file and get a new hold on life! You might even decide to "dump" a go nowhere relationship whether it is an employer or business partner and move forward towards something more positive for you.

JUST LET GO!

When you think about it, you actually can do all of the things you want to do, by starting right now and listening to what you tell yourself. If you want to do something, go ahead and tell your brain what you want to do but be ready to put things in motion...your brain will remember where you left off until you complete the task! We are already doing just that when we plan our vacations each year. The first thing we do is sit down and decide where you really want to go. Then you ponder how you want to arrive at your destination. Will it be a cruise or cross country driving, or will you fly? Then you calculate the cost. Next you may have to work overtime, or budget a credit card to pay for the trip in advance and if you have an employer, you schedule that time for vacation! Viola! It is done!

The brain never troubles you about the trip again until the calendar reminds you it is almost time to start packing and you are off! In each area of our lives we can control what we do by first listening to what we tell ourselves we want or don't want. If you have negative behaviors, attitudes, thoughts or perceptions, you can discard them just as easily! Scientist are not completely clear as to why humans choose to hold on to every negative thing they encounter instead of just letting some things go. The good news is, there are millions of people that are learning how to take control of their brains every day. This next overview gives us various ways to look at how complex our brains are and how our environment can make or break us depending on the information we are fed... Do you feel you are overweight and are not sure why, if there are no medical reasons to cause it? Could it be a toxic relationship? A bad experience from the past? A trauma? A present situation you are in and you don't know how to get out of it? What about something that happened from childhood that you are still holding onto? Let's look at a scenario about a woman who had issues from childhood and see how her brain processed some of the data she had been fed and now was feeding herself.

JUST LET GO!

Overeating and Brain Control

One woman named Jody, stated in an interview during our research on this subject of hoarding negative behaviors and thoughts; "I was overeating every day until one day I tipped the scale at 250 lbs. I was so disgusted at myself that I sat and cried for hours, while consuming a full pack of Oreo cookies and dunking each of them neatly in a glass of milk. I felt worse after eating all those cookies than I did before I started. I began thinking and researching how the brain works. I listened to tapes, watched videos and by the time I was finished, I realized something that had happened to me from childhood. I remembered never getting to eat all of the goodies I wanted, when I wanted as a child. As an adult, I was able to eat anything I enjoyed and could do so at will. I realized I had developed a negative habit of "overeating" out of the thought that I could now eat whatever I wanted and no one would tell me I couldn't!

So I ate anytime, anywhere. After gaining all the weight and being irresponsible with my freedom of choice, I told myself that I would "change my mind" on how I looked at this new found "freedom" of making my own choices. It made all the difference in the world! I realized I didn't have to eat everything I wanted every day because I had the power to decide "when" I wanted something and I knew I could have it! I had to tell my "Brain" that I could make the decision to have whatever I wanted and didn't have to force feed myself to prove that point anymore. To me, it was as simple as that. Coupled with exercise and balancing my meals, I honestly examined "why" I was doing what I did and then changed my thinking. I talked to myself first and was able to let go of my childhood fear of being "denied" something I wanted." I lost 80lbs and now look and feel amazing! **Janice M**.

JUST LET GO!

This woman is like many people. She is taking back control of her thoughts from childhood. No longer living off old memories and habits that were predicated on a lack of knowledge and understanding as a child. She viewed her weight gain in a different manner as an adult and realizes that "her thoughts" were the culprit of this dilemma of obesity. Her parents didn't allow her to overeat as a child, but she viewed this as being "denied" something she wanted which was simply to make her own choices. However, now an adult and after gaining weight and examining her motives for eating, she realized that she always had the power to make her own "choices" of when, what and how much to eat. This woman honestly examined her mind and heart for the answers she sought. Once she was clear, she told her brain what she wanted "it" to do. By working along with those thoughts she was able to drop the weight she had put on over the years.

She said she also had never liked the word diet because the letters in the word represented to her "**D**id **I** **E**at **T**oday," which always reminded her that she was hungry. Most people do not like thinking that they are doing something that the first three letters in the word is **DIE!** Strange but negatively true. So, why do so many negative things we experience stay with us for such a long time? This is because we simply do not know how to identify the true cause of the negatives we harbor and "WHERE" to DUMP" the MENTAL WASTE we carry. That's right! Even our brains yearn to dump stuff out of it because "it" realizes there is no use for "IT." Many times we say thing such as, "I want to get something off my chest!" What you are really saying is, you want to get something off your "mind," which has travelled to your chest screaming for relief!

This is called "anxiety!" That heavy feeling that if not addressed and released can make you physically sick. The brain can only hold things for so long when it's overloaded. Then it MUST DUMP things and will "spill" the beans of toxic mental waste stored. Sadly, many go on *hoarding* negative thoughts until their brain is clogged with mental trash that it is now forced to dump out in pieces when something "jars" or provokes you.

JUST LET GO!

Whatever toxic mind waste is prevalent in your brain, this is what is used to fuel unnecessary arguments, snapping off on people for no reason, destroying good relationships for all the wrong reasons, making poor decisions and aging before your time. All of this is based on how you feel about something at that moment rather than the practical thought of what is needed. This could be in the form of a bedtime argument that creeps in from nowhere. When you see this happening, know that something has "triggered" you. Own up to the fact that there is something on your mind that is bothering you! Find out what it is…and address it! When you talk about something over and over, it takes the sting out of it and eventually the brain sees no reason to bring it up because "you" have brought it up relentlessly. The brain also gets bored with the same thing over and over. Stop masking thoughts or feelings you may have. Bring them out in the open. A trigger is your brains way of trying to get your attention to handle things that make you uncomfortable. Get things off your chest and free up your thoughts and relieve undue anxiety! Many times we feel guilty even talking to someone else about how we really feel inside because the feelings are so TOXIC. ...See how this scenario plays out....

 **Just Let GO**

> A "TOXIC" MIND IS A TERRIBLE THING…SO WASTE IT!!!

There was a woman who stated; "I can always listen to my friends and family's problems, but when I try to vent to them, they all cringe and look at me like I have two heads and both heads are wearing different hats! I couldn't understand why no one could take the pressure of hearing me vent when I could listen to them all day…and offer suggestions to help.

JUST LET GO!

*Finally, the woman realized the issue after many years of experiencing this. She accepted that what was in her mind was so **toxic**, that other people were repelled by it! She finally came to grips with her situation of being violated as a child and when she was ready to release the information from her brain to free herself of feeling like a victim, she thought she had someone to release this information to, but it was not received well by the people she chose to with. The people didn't know how to accept what she told them because they had issues of their own, unknown to the woman telling the experience.*

They had been using "her" to satisfy some of "their" toxic releases which was going well for them and they had become accustomed to the woman being there for "them." The fact is, they would never be able to support her because they feared "the woman" would no longer be there for "them" to dump their troubles on. So, when the woman would begin venting to her friends, "their" already clogged brains simply "stopped listening." Ultimately, the woman acquired a new set of friends in her circle and was able to gradually resolve some of the issues she previously had. She learned that before she dumped on random people, she sought individuals that she "knew" could handle her experience and the emotions tied to it.

The woman was very successful and found relief in sharing with her new circle of friends. She felt ever more positive when she let go of those individuals who had only pretended to be there for her in order to monopolize her time and brain cells selfishly. Although, they were helping themselves with her ability to listen to them, they never had any interest in ever giving anything back to her. Now, when she wanted to discuss concerns she had that were deep, she sought out those individuals that were there to support her in a positive way. In time, the woman became more positive. She had to "Just let go" of the negative relationships she had acquired over the years that were only one way and gave nothing back to her in return for her absorbing all of their negative data.

JUST LET GO!

Remember that many people have experienced this type of issue with so called friends. Know that true friends are always there for you. If you have friends that cannot be there for you, realize that they too may have negatives they are trying to "dump," as well. Now when you see this type of reaction you will know that something else is going on within them. They may not be doing this on purpose, but desperately trying to rid themselves of the pain of carrying around negative baggage of their own. However, while you can help in some situations, never allow yourself to become the waste dump for other people's negativity especially if you have negatives of your own that need to be released. Test the waters to see if those friends can support you, if not, find those that can!

If you have friends who only call you when their spouse or significant other is away, examine the relationship, there may be something else to this behavior. It could be jealousy or a troubled relationship and a need to show undivided attention to a jealous mate. If you find it's neither, then you are their DUMPING ground! You may want to be "unavailable" sometimes when this happens in order not to become loaded down with other peoples' problems. Have you had a friend or family member with so many problems that when they call, you have to put them on "MUTE" in order to stay on the phone to keep your blood pressure down? In these instances, tell the caller you will get back to them. If it's that bad, write them a letter or send a card to see how they are doing or if you do occasionally take their call, time yourself and politely hang up before it begins to affect you. These are "toxic" conversations that are not health and can keep you awake at night.

For this reason, be careful what you allow people to "confide" to you. The brain holds this data and if it's too sensitive, it makes you "responsible" for doing something with the information. These toxic relationships reap no benefits except to beget more negative feelings to clog your own mind! Analyze your life and relationships carefully and see clearly what's clogging your brain with negative emotions and feelings you may be concealing.

JUST LET GO!

Another thing to consider is to stop trying "not" to hurt people's feelings all the while allowing yours to be trampled on! It is okay to say, "that's enough" or, "No!" Learn to use these statements when needed and do this with the greatest of ease. These are some reason why we should learn to "Just Let Go!" Carrying around excess negative baggage comes in all shapes, sizes and situations. Negatives can stay hidden until they refuse to stay in and simply "pop" out at the most inopportune times. Our bodies are naturally designed to *expel* anything it doesn't need. When we get a cold, we have the sniffles. When we eat or drink too much, we visit the restroom. When our ears need to be cleaned, a neat ball of wax falls out in the strangest places. So you would agree that if your brain is too full, "it" too will find a way to "*dump*" some of the mental *waste it **doesn't** need* to relieve the pressure! *So what's next?*

"REMOVE UNECESSARY PRESSURE"

We know that repetition is good for memory. So…have you ever had a *panic attack*? Did you go to the hospital thinking you were dying? Once there, you immediately calmed down knowing you were where you would be cared for and the anxiety subsided? Panic attacks happen when the mind and body has been overloaded! *However,* when we remove ourselves from the source of mental overload, our brain breathes a sigh of relief. Negative thoughts can be like a pair of a too-tight jeans. They can rob us of the comfort and enjoyment of the moment, all for the sake of looking good. How often do we hide our true feelings in public about someone or something and then go home in private and cry? If this is what you do, you must develop the new habit of letting go of things that cause you pain even momentarily and replace it with things, thoughts, behaviors and perceptions that truly make you feel happy!

JUST LET GO!

We are not saying you should lie to yourself about anything, but try to keep a positive outlook rather than a negative one. What's the next step? We have now looked at a few powers to use for letting go of negative thinking. Before we delve into the subject at large for the last ones, a good eye opener is to identify a small list of negative things you may be holding onto which could be building up "***Toxic***" mental waste in your brain. Make a short list of 5 things that could be sapping your ***positive energy*** with negative thoughts, attitudes perceptions or behaviors. Think before you make your short list and start with the smallest things and work your way up. Don't take the list lightly!

JUST LET GO LIST

1.

2.

3.

4.

5.

JUST LET GO!

You can always change it when you have "DUMPED" these first 5 things that may be clogging your brain. It could be something you need to do, but be honest and give yourself permission to say what is truly on your mind. When you have completed the list, relax, read a good book and find out what caused you to not address these things before now. Take a drive out in the country. Go to the beach...whatever you do, think openly, honestly and go all the way back to your childhood if need be. Now that you've made a short list, remember, this is just the first step to removing something negative from your brain. Writing things down and addressing them one by one is also powerful! In most cases, thoughts are subliminal until they materialize by way of a behavior, attitude, perception or "*TRIGGERS!*

Think about this...When was the last time you looked into your brain? Exactly! If we could see the negative garbage in it, the inclination would be to turn it upside down and dump it out the same as you would do if you had sand in your shoes. It would be a no brainer. We only see the negative effects of what happens in our brain when the negatives have taken full control of our lives and we become the "puppet" and our negative thoughts become the puppeteer. Left unchecked, the "Puppeteer" can become sinister and our thoughts could destroy our self-worth, self-esteem and ultimately our happiness. Now, let's talk about letting something go! The first thing that comes to mind when we consider letting something go is when "it" is too heavy to carry. None of us think our lives are too heavy to carry because we can't see what we are carrying in our heads that weighing us down.

Letting go can be in a physical or mental form, whether small or large. Biting ones fingernails down to the quick could be something small, yet there is an underlying reason why you do it. On the other hand, getting out of an abusive relationship is more of a significant challenge. You may need more mental power to "Just Let Go" of a relationship that doesn't work! Either of these issues, if left unchecked can become potentially dangerous to us over time. One example that comes to mind is that of; letting go of a live electrical wire or a red hot poker! Now, this is farfetched, but you get the point.

JUST LET GO!

You wouldn't pick these things up in the first place if you are smart. But, certainly if you had one in your hand for good reason and it began heating up, you would quickly "Let It Go!" No questions about it. It would be common sense to do so. As we alluded to earlier, this point can also apply to relationships we have with others that for one reason or another become "toxic or too "heavy" to carry. When this happens, it may be time to let go. This statement is not suggesting throwing away a relationship of any sort that might have sustained some trouble from time to time. This is expected in life, marriage or business arrangements. This is only an example of areas that could become toxic or too heavy to carry physically or mentally, and when you identify this, you must examine if you should "just let it go."

It is time to take action to remove negative patterns of thinking! Even when we hold onto old ideas or habits that don't work for us, they too can clog our ability to stay "light" mentally. We should now be ready to embrace new thoughts and ideas which keep us mentally and physically vibrant and moving in a positive direction. Beware of what is happening in your life, especially if you are surrounded by negatively charged people. These types of situations will reveal themselves clearly over time as to the validity in our lives. Remember, life is a "job." If we get up every day, we are alive! That means, we have to "work" at staying that way. Therefore, we must feed, clothe, medicate, amuse, clean, rest and entertain ourselves daily. When we feed our bodies, we must also feed our "mind" or it will starve to death! Life constitutes "Work!" So, remember that it requires action 24/7.

Recall, when we "recognize" that something is too heavy for us to bear, we should develop the habit and the power to "Just Let Go!" It may not happen overnight, but if we focus on what we want to let go of and write it down and work on each area one step at a time. With support, continual effort, letting go of negatives will happen.

JUST LET GO!

Many of us have gotten good at ignoring our inner voice. But remember, that voice is your brain talking to you! If our inner voice is tuned properly, over time, we learn how to make positive adjustments to our decisions when something isn't working for us. We have been taught that if we "change our mind" about something, we are being indecisive. That's not true! Changing your mind only means that you have reconsidered a decision you made in haste or in the absence of information you didn't have to make the best decision from the beginning! That is why in relationships, pre-nuptials are in place for some. We also have to learn to give ourselves "permission" to let go of negatives.

We may find "letting go" difficult because of outdated belief systems handed down to us from various cultural trends or even superstitions. Many people don't even believe in what was handed down to them...they just go along with it because mom, dad, grandma and grandpa, did it! They feel an obligation to carry a valueless tradition to their graves with no sensible explanation as to whether it has positively affected their lives. Furthermore, there is no guarantee it will positively affect the future lives of those who might inherit it from you. So why pay it forward? Instead of letting it go and adopting a new approach that will have a positive outcome, many simply pass on to their children; unfounded thoughts and harmful beliefs.

The goal here is to identify things that are good to pass on and those that are not! We can do this by removing the unnecessary "negatives" from our thoughts and behaviors daily. A simple mental attitude adjustment could relieve physical, emotional and psychological nuances. The point is to systematically balance the weight we take on physically and mentally each day in order to sustain the wear and tear that naturally occurs within us over time.

JUST LET GO!

Since Letting Go is a heavy subject, and we want to "lighten" up a bit on the brain, we'll use a simple explanation of how to view this. We will start by looking at views of Men and Women and how they differ on the subject of "WEIGHT," and carrying something too heavy. Are men smarter than women when it comes to this subject? No…just different. We will use physical "weight" as the object for our brains and see how this pans out. Let's see how the sexes differ and how this mindset can be affecting our brains. When you see how "weight" is viewed by men and women, you may see the disparity in how we manage many of our affairs in life.

MEN vs. WOMEN ON CARRYING EXCESS WEIGHT

We've all heard that women are from Venus and men are from Mars. Or, is it the other way around? Who really cares? The fact is that men and women *are* as different as the planets they are supposed to represent. It is the same when it comes to carrying heavy objects or picking up things too heavy to carry. Women are said to be "natural" nurturers and beautiful creatures of habit. They often carry many weighty things around in life and are accustomed to doing so. They carry extra body weight from being pregnant. Then, they physically carry the babies after delivery along with all other things they need. They carry the burdens of rearing children in many households. They work jobs that may weigh them down mentally and physically.

The stresses in life for women in this century seem to far outweigh the stresses of their male counterparts. But is this because all of these things have been heaped upon women? No! It is mostly by choice! Women, choose many of the things they encounter in life. Does it have to be that way? No! Women sometimes carry unnecessary burdens around along with the weight of things they do not want or need. However, they sometimes hold on to things they should let go of for obvious reasons but they don't!

JUST LET GO!

Over time, they wonder why they are stressed or depressed. It's hard for women to let things go because they are taught to "support." We don't want to get too deep so let's use a simple analogy of women carrying too much weight around. Case and point; "A woman's purse!" The proverbial nap sack, backpack, medicine cabinet, makeup kit, diaper bag, you name it, the purse is the bag of the day! The problem is, women carry too many things "in" their purses. These things weigh them down physically and mentally. One woman, the mother of three children, was asked why she carried so many things in her purse and she simple stated, "in case someone needs something!" "REALLY!!!" As a fact, the majority of women carry too many things in their purses for the same reasons, "in case they need something!" They are doing themselves a horrible disservice of trying to be prepared for the next "anything!" Everything they have in their purse, they believe they "need." (A mini form of hoarding). Just saying…

This becomes their justification for keeping these and other items on their person as if the Let's Make A Deal host, will stop them on the street and give them cash if they can show him a strand of yak hair! If the likelihood of seeing the host would actually happen on a daily basis, having all these things in the purse for that reason might make sense. However, unless you are on his show, you won't be needing yak hair! And yet, some women continue to carry everything around! The first thing women do when they hoist their purses onto their shoulders is to adjust it. Especially if they have to walk for any distance.

The purses today are outrageously large and usually can take up a passenger seat. Some purses are so full that their owners can't close them and end up leaving them gaped open for the world to look inside! So, what is the real deal with women carrying so many things in their purses? They are "conditioned" to do so! Can they be cured of this bad habit? "Yes!" Take a look at this scenario and see if it fits you or someone you know.

JUST LET GO!

Just Let GO

CAUTION...PURSE TOO HEAVY

A woman entered her vehicle one day to go shopping. While discharging her purse on the front passenger seat, she noticed a faint yellow light that illuminated on the dash board. Initially, she did not know why the light was on because she had never seen it before. Being very cautious about maintaining her vehicle, she wondered if everything was okay and made one last attempt to determine why the strange light was on. Looking over every inch of her vehicle she found nothing. Still unsatisfied, she scanned the car like an unemployed detective. Finally, with further inspection, she noticed the small writing on the illuminated dashboard. Squinting to read the small inscription, she dug in her oversized purse for a pair of glasses. She realized it was the "child safety" warning sensor light which had been activated. But, "why?" While vaguely confused, knowing there were no children in the car with her, she instinctively looked in horror at the passenger seat and......there it was!

Now it was clear why the light had come on. She had dropped her "purse" on the front passenger seat which had activated the child safety sensor! She normally dropped her purse on the floor of the car. But today, she was in a hurry and the purse was exceptionally heavy. She had added bottles of water to it for her work out later. The vehicle weight sensor light came on when it recognized a "weight" in the passenger seat that was heavy enough to be deemed a "passenger, but not heavy enough to qualify being in the front seat because of the weight requirement. The sensor had done its job to warn the driver to place the child or "object" in this case, her "purse," in the back seat for safety! The woman was flabbergasted! She sat in her driveway shaking her head in disbelief, now looking at her purse as if it were a monster.

JUST LET GO!

Still unsatisfied about what had just happened, she wanted to satisfy her own thoughts about the potential weight she was carrying so she flipped through her purse. She wanted to see what had really caused the sensor to go off. Surely it couldn't be her purse? She thought. Upon inspection, she noted there was nothing in the seat but the purse and low and behold, she began pulling items out one by one. Shock and shame set in all at once as she piled items in the seat filling it up. She noted...charging cords for her iPad and speakers. A huge makeup bag, a comb, brush set, a pair of socks, a scarf, wallet, which was needed but it had six check books in it with dental floss, two cell phones, gum, (bulk pack), 2 bottles of lotion, eye drops, band aids, tooth picks, hand wipes and a bottle of sanitizer, a book, sun glasses and two pairs of reading glasses including the pair she had on...and the list went on!"

The woman shook her head in disbelief that day and vowed to change her bad habit of carrying unnecessary things around with her from that moment forward. She finally started her car to continue to her destination. She vowed that she would begin the process of changing a bad habit by replacing her oversized purse with a "smaller" one. When she got back to her car from shopping, she didn't wait for another minute to go by without making the change right then and there. She emptied over half or more of the items from her old purse to the new smaller one.

The woman drove back home a happier and much "lighter" woman. From time to time, she glanced in her rear view mirror looking at the "old" huge purse laying on the seat, lifeless. It was faded and stretched out of shape from being stuffed with too many things over its lifetime. Going forward, she reasoned that if she needed anything extra, she would fit in in the glove compartment but would also monitor that behavior to keep from hoarding in her car! She now understood how removing items from one area to another could also become a negative habit and could get out of hand very quickly! What happened to this woman could happen to anyone.

JUST LET GO!

This woman is like many who carry unnecessary things around with them. Only when something "triggers" our brain to stop a negative behavior is when we will actually do something about it. Once we recognize the "trigger," we can "react" in a positive way to fix it! For this woman, it was the "child sensor" safety light in her car that illuminated and helped her recognize that she was carrying "excess weight." If we start with the small things, we can tackle the bigger ones as we move forward! Look over the list of 5 things you have annotated earlier and soon you can let go of some simple negative behaviors, and clear out something on your to-do list. If you think your purse is too heavy…remove half of what's in it and only keep what you absolutely need. Keys, a checkbook, a tube of lipstick, cellphone, wallet.

Keep a small travel pack in your glove compartment if you need additional things. A small umbrella on the door of each vehicle. Anything else can probably wait. Remember, only take what you will need for the trip! This may not be you, but if you know someone who does have this problem of carrying way too many things in their purses share this story with them! Stop carrying around things that weigh you down whether the weight is in your mind or in your purse! "Just Let Go!"

"It's not the FUTURE we are afraid of. It's repeating the PAST that makes us anxious."
~Unknown~

JUST LET GO!

MEN "PICKING UP" HEAVY OBJECTS

We read the scenario about how women will sometimes "carry" excess weight in their purses until they see the "light." But are men any different when it comes to carrying heavy things? ""Yes!" Men are simplistic when it comes to carrying things around that are too heavy. They choose to carry only what they need on their person. They will not carry anything on them that can't fit in their back or front pockets or would cause an unusual protrusions. You normally do not see men with bulging pockets. If you do, please write in and let us know. If you check a man's pockets, you will find a few of these simple items depending on what he is doing and what kind of pants he is wearing. A wallet, some keys, perhaps spare pocket change, and an occasional chap stick…we call it, (man rouge). Why they need that…no one knows, but we'll let them have it.

The fact is, a chap stick is lighter than a tube of lip stick for women. Go figure! If a man has something he doesn't want to carry, he will usually give it to someone else to lug around. Whether it's his wife, girlfriend, sister, or whoever has the largest bag… they are "IT" for carrying the item. If a man has to carry something, it will be for short stents. He will find a way to dump it because men want to be as "free" as possible. Don't ask a man to carry anything other than his child, or his thoughts because he doesn't want to do it. It upsets his psyche.

JUST LET GO!

However, there is one giant flaw in the man category of picking up and carrying heavy things. We accept that they carry only what they need on their person. However, if you see a man in the gym, he will strain every muscle, vein and artery in his body to lift 300 lbs. of dead weight to impress his friends, his lady or his peers. Don't ask him why! No one really knows. It doesn't make sense to me either but we all know it's true. They will also carry their women over the threshold, pick them up on the beach, or even carry them over puddles of water. (I've heard of that happening). Most men's emotions are simple and uncluttered as well. Consider this case and point. They can "Let Go" of anything, to include a relationship after they leave the room they are in with a person or thing that bogs them down mentally or physically.

They can forget about the person cold turkey! No theme song, no Rocky Road ice cream to mourn the lost relationship. They just LET GO! It's as simple as that. It doesn't mean that all men are cold hearted. Most are loving creatures and great to have around. This simply means that they do not prefer to carry around anything that bogs them down. If they feel that something is excessive whether it is a conversation or someone's outfit, they can walk away from it and flip it off and "Let It Go! Men prefer picking up dead weight that they know they can "drop" quickly because they are not "required to carry it around forever." They only want to know that they "can" pick up the weighty things in life when it is necessary or if they want to impress someone to include themselves. Picking up weight has to have a purpose.

A bit narcissistic if you ask me, but…oh well! They are geared to take care of the "weightier" matters in situations and will "Just Let everything else Go" in life. Ladies, that's a good life lesson to adopt. The unnecessary weight women carry around forces them to become weighed down and ineffective at times when it is necessary to solve heavy problems in life. That doesn't mean women are slow mentally, or incapable! On the contrary! But they should consider only picking up those weighty things when they "absolutely need to!" Other than that, if it's too heavy to jog around the block with it…do like the guys do and "Just Let Go!"

JUST LET GO!

"DO YOU WANT TO CHANGE?"

Only you can determine when change will take place in your life. When you accept that you have developed bad habits that may be hindering your happiness, the "next" step is to learn how to make the necessary change to move forward. For those who truly have had enough of the madness of holding onto negative behaviors and thoughts, they soon become willing participants and muster up the courage to turn the pages in their lives to experience greater success of living. If you want to change, you must examine the problems you are experiencing and accept that you must rid yourself of anything that leaves you "empty" at the end of the day! Wipe the slate clean and begin again with a fresh approach what's important to you! Everything we've discussed is geared to help you identify some negative areas that you may want to change by seeing how others have fared in the same process of living with various negativity! Agree that "TODAY," you will allow your mind's eye to be opened to new ideas and thoughts about making a positive change. You will learn how to live a better life by taking charge of the one you have right now! Ask yourself some important questions before moving on!

JUST LET GO!

Questions to Ask Yourself

1) Do I have negative feelings from an old relationship?
2) Am I jealous or envious of mom, sister, friends, workmates, daughters, uncles, dad, brother, in-laws or someone else?
3) Do I have superstitious beliefs about securing life insurance for myself or loved ones?
4) Do I get angry when things don't go my way?
5) Do I hold back showing love or affection due to guilt or shame because of something that happened years ago?
6) Am I angry with someone else and take it out on those that are near me that are not to blame?
7) Do I have phobias that prevent me from doing things I want to do such as flying, riding a train, or taking long road trips?
8) Do I have a need to control others?
9) Do I avoid hugging or being close to others even if they are family?
10) Do I put off things I need to do out of fear or frustration?
11) Do I think I am not smart enough to get what I want?
12) Do I believe I am fat or ugly?
13) Do I allow people to put me down or take advantage of me?

JUST LET GO!

Once you have pondered these question or have other specific questions not listed, "write them down!" It's time to delve into the specifics of the "whys" when it comes to negative baggage in our lives. It is time to **"JUST LET GO,"** of anything that doesn't fit in your life to make you happy! We will walk through the next few pages of the book and glean nuggets of gold to help clear our heads of debris we have collected over the years. The subjects covered in this book are only the beginning…there is more to come, but let's begin here, shall we?

"Stop Allowing People or Things to Control You!"

This is one area of power many people must learn to take back. Allowing others to control us will inevitably cause undue stress and anxiety at some point in our lives if we allow unnecessary control of ourselves. As reasoning adults, we should have the desire and the willpower to make certain decisions for ourselves. For those who are truly incapable of doing so on their own…i.e., children, aging family members or disabled individuals, we certainly can accept the limitations there. However, when we think about something or someone controlling us, we should always examine our values and assess the things we have learned or have been handed down from generations. Many times we do things by rote. Meaning that we were told to think and act a certain way and that's what we did as children without thinking. If we find ourselves doing this as adults, that's a problem. However, many have found that their lives have been drastically altered in an unproductive way when they focus on things they have been handed down that no longer fit their lives in a positive way. Now it's time to take back the control of your mind in order to get ready to make new decisions that fit the time you are living in. One way to begin this process is by examining things you've learned from watching examples that were set for you in life. This is not to take anything away from the good old way of doing basic things, but some things simply "need" changing! Let's see how we will begin.

JUST LET GO
of
Superstitions

What's the thought about having to "chip in" when someone "checks out?

For all humans and animals, survival is a universal quest. The main goal for each of us is to make it from one day to the next. We are so sincere about surviving that sometimes people may inadvertently alter the way they think about how they might prolong their existence. Some believe that by avoiding things like buying a life insurance policy can somehow extend their longevity. Or, by avoiding discussing the thought that someday... life as we know it will end for us before we achieve any or all of our goals we've set for ourselves and our family. Some have believed things they learned as children, thinking that by some strange phenomenon, if they had no burial policies for themselves they would somehow escape the inevitable. Others may feel that they can't afford insurance and do not put it on their high priority list.

Either way, there are many negative superstitious beliefs and myths that have been handed down to people from all walks of life. Granted, most people do not think that way today and ensure that they are protected, but there are still those who are caught without insurance for various reasons that cost family members and clergy a lot of unnecessary grief. When this happens, it may put the family in a whirl spin and this is where, "chipping in," gets serious! Many young adults are striking out on their own earlier in life and life insurance may be the last thing they think of before they get their apartment, car, and other necessities.

JUST LET GO!

They may not think about the "what if's" in life as older adults may, but since we are creatures of habits, we will usually follow the examples that have been set for us during childhood. If you heard conversations from your parents about life insurance premiums and policies when you were growing up, those conversations may be recalled and cause you to be more apt to ensure that you have a policy of your own when you choose to leave home.

While everyone that does not have insurance is not superstitious, the thought of not having a policy should not make anyone feel excluded from the inevitable. It is the same mindset with saving money and other such important positive habits that must be developed early in life. We must learn to develop our own belief systems. If the ones we grew up with are not working for us in that we are well rounded in our thinking we must change! Because of some deep seated beliefs, some people may still refuse to secure a life policy for themselves and will not allow anyone else to pay for one for them. This is where change must take place. If you have such feelings, remember that a policy of any kind is a positive "protection" for your loved ones not a burden. It has nothing to do with speeding up or slowing down your own demise once it is in force.

This type of belief is the worst of its kind! It surpasses, the black cat crossing your path, walking under a ladder, breaking a mirror and the list goes on. These types of negative thoughts lack purpose. Many families become financially depleted during an already troubled economic time when someone checks out and there is nothing in place to care for their final expenses. Sometimes negative beliefs and habits are handed down to us like a father's inheritance to his child.

   Just Let GO

www.victoriaekain.com

JUST LET GO!

However, in the end, a real but "unnecessary" fear was created in many young minds. What can the effects of a negative mindset do to people? It can destroy a person's happiness. Any negative beliefs, solely based on superstitious data can become a stumbling block as well. In the end, if not altered, negatives will be handed down to family members which could create a chain reaction.

When you think of superstitions, think of this. There are many people today that are afraid to do simple things such as traveling for long distances by car or flying for the first time. Many may attempt to combat their fear of flying by getting into their vehicles and speeding down highways as a way to prove that they are not afraid of speed, but it still does not take away that true fear that they possess. In this instance, a truly morbid fear exists. Do you still throw salt over your shoulder, or become afraid of a black cat simply crossing your path going his merry way?

When we think back to the "chipping in" for a loved one's final expenses, has this become the uncanny norm? People are losing their homes because they are having to skip their mortgage or rent payments to "chip in." It is not to say that if they don't or can't "chip in" the departed was not loved! It simply means that most families are hit by economic hardship and are already struggling to stay afloat and have not planned for expenses outside of their own personal budgets.

Many have turned to their clergy who is eager to assist, but it still places an unfortunate burden on others to make these arrangements for services. But is heaping this type of burden on individuals a true show of love? Every time this happens, without realizing it, some family members feel the pressure to try to give more than others, but hard times are hitting everyone.

JUST LET GO!

With this said, the real solution is simple. Everyone should budget for a simple LIP (Life Insurance Policy) that someone or several people might agree to pay on for the family's needs if they cannot afford it. This is all that is required. The suggestion here is that family members should consider the strain this encroaching process puts on loved ones when everyone has to "continually" chip in to pay for expenses they have not been personally budgeted for. So if you believe that "not having a policy for yourself will cause you to live longer" if that were the case, no one on this earth would ever own one!!! We'd all like to live on for an eternity.

It was stated that "bad" things happen all the time unexpectedly along with things that "people" sometimes cause themselves. At this point, we must dispel "all" superstitious beliefs in order to move forward in a positive way! No one can "Rest in Peace" when the family is fighting and arguing because there may not be enough money to pay for the services for a family member. Let's look at a couple who had the right mindset when it came to planning a family vacation. This should be the "norm" of attitudes.

Just Let GO

JUST LET GO!

"A Positive View of Life"

A couple and their four children were travelling to see the grandparents one summer. Since they all were travelling together, the mother realized they all would be travelling together so she determined that she would contact their insurance agent and annotated their Life insurance policies and changed beneficiaries. She and her husband agreed that in the event of anything happening to "all" of them, during the trip, they selected "temporary," beneficiaries for the duration of their vacation. Once they returned safely home...."which they did," the temporary beneficiaries were automatically revoked. They had a beautiful vacation visiting their family and nothing happened to them. Many years went by after their vacation and the family is still healthy and happy! It was as simple as that! When the young couple was asked why they did what they did before their trip, the woman stated "I didn't want my mother and father fretting about anything if something should befall us that was out of our control while we travelled."

She further stated, "I felt it would be more tragic to have the grandparents "burdened" with going to court in another state to unravel the mess of not being able to take possession of our property legally to close out our affairs if an accident had happened. Since there would have been two sets of grandparents surviving, both sides may have had different thoughts and beliefs about what should take place which could have gotten messy if things were not spelled out. She simply stated, "I love my family and always consider them first. We didn't want anyone to have to "chip" in for something my husband and I were responsible for." J. Johns

This family's conviction is one that is well worth accepting at some point in our lives. Having their family protected did not stop them from "Living" their lives and taking a family vacation and enjoying themselves.

JUST LET GO!

This couple was not in fear of losing their life because the policy was in place. They felt confident that in the event they needed it, it would protect the loved ones left behind. They didn't simply let the thought of "doom" take over them and enjoyed their time away. This is a beautiful example of how we "all" should feel about our loved ones and about life. We should not want to leave our family or clergy scrambling to pay for our expenses from an already stretched budget. Some family members have needed to take out high interest bank loans. Some even pull from their rent and have lost their leases because of it. Sadly, in situations where there is no one to front the funds needed for these expenses, a pauper's final service may be provided.

Now is the time to "Just let go" of superstitious thinking. STOP delaying!!! Life is hard enough for most people without the added burdens! Be sensible!

JUST LET GO!

We all wish those who have taken that journey the most "peaceful" rest. But chipping in can take a toll on a family very quickly if not corrected. In some cases, when entire families have this mindset of not thinking ahead for these times, it keeps the negative thoughts and financial burdens alive in many households and should be halted! Why do so many fear the inevitable? How can we get past the morbid fear of this type of thinking? We may have become comfortable not having to change the way we think because it feels too much like "work" to change our minds about something we don't even understand. It is easy to say that we did something because our parents and grandparents did it whether we agreed with it or not. It may be harder coming up with our own ideas about how things should work for us if it's not our routine way of thinking.

On this subject of chipping in when someone checks out, remember that it only hurts the family when plans are not in place for the inevitable. If the thought of that still bothers you, start an emergency fund and put a trusted person over it. Only put in it what you know you will need and nothing more. Think about it…family members would rather have "you" than any funds you would leave behind. In the meantime, Just Let Go, of superstitious thinking! "Live life, love and be happy." Take a vacation or do things you've always wanted to do. Everything else will take care of itself! JUST LET GO of negative habits.

Don't Get Caught in a Net of Superstitions

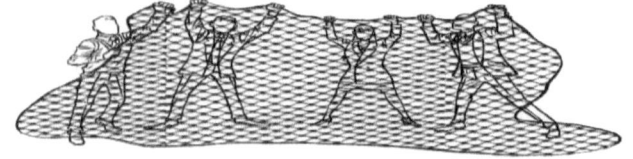

JUST LET GO
of
Bad Habits

Everyone develops a bad habit or two in their lifetime. The fact is, it's hard to drop a "bad habit" once you pick it up. It's even more difficult to pick one out as an example that might fit the masses, but here goes...Let's try this one; If you are of average adult age, you have "bills," it's the American way. Everyone gets bills in the mail, so what do you do when you go to the mail box each day? Do you pick up your mail and sort it and put it away to reconcile it later? Or, do you do like many people, and carry your bills around with you even when you are not paying them? Do you put them in your purse, laundry room, kitchen, shelf or your vehicle?

Do you take them to work and put them in your drawer? How about this? Do you put them in the garage when you get them out of your mailbox and leave them there to collect dust? Or, do you put them all over your house and hunt for them when it's time to pay a bill? If you do this, the good news is, you are normal! The bad news is, you've developed a bad habit. Have you ever asked yourself why you leave your bills everywhere? What was your answer? In researching this matter, many people had the same habit of putting their bills everywhere. Secretly they wanted them to disappear. It's not likely that someone was going to steal the bills and pay them. Even if they were stolen, who in their right mind would press charges? Some people have different ways they pay bills. Some people go to each place where they have accounts and pay with cash.

Others stated they kept bills in their purses, or vehicles. Some stated that they take them to work so they can pay them online during their lunch hour because when they get home, they are too tired. These are good points to consider, but think about the horrible habit you have of carrying around bills, and paid receipts. This is a bad habit that should be broken immediately!

JUST LET GO!

Have you ever gone out to eat and reached in your purse for your wallet and a utility bill fell out? It's embarrassing to say the least. Or you open your car door and the pocket on the door is full of old receipts. There are two trains of thought about "letting go," of this bad habit. First, if this habit is something you learned from someone, this may be why you have followed the same course of action. If you learned this from a parent, you must realize that your parents may have had their bills with them because technology was not what it is today. Good news! In this century, you can pay a bill from your iPhone. This habit can go away with a few simple changes made to your routine each day. Second, remember that everything we learn can be "unlearned." If you carry your bills around, ask yourself "why?" If the answer makes no sense, stop the habit immediately! We know habits are hard to break but this one could cost you dearly. A simple way to break this habit is to set some guidelines for your mail and follow through. If you are tired of wading through purses, car doors, drawers, the garage and other places for bills you must pay, such as mortgage, water, light, gas, cable, phone or pest control, try the suggestions below, it could mean the difference in lights on or lights off.

HOW TO HALT PUTTING BILLS EVERYWHERE

(1) Designate a primary and secondary person to get all mail from the mailbox
(2) Agree to put all mail in ONE place.
(3) Create a MAIL center. Take three shoe boxes, keep in this order and label (INCOMING, PAY, REVIEW, TRASH,)
(4) Trash all sales ads that clutter your mail box if you are budgeting.
(5) Choose a day of the week to READ and distribute all mail and stick to it.
(6) Never get the mail from the mail box when you are pulling out of your driveway. People find mail in their garage, on top of the washer and dryer, on the potato bin, kitchen counters, in drawers or anywhere there is a surface.
(7) Never discuss bills in bed, at dinner or when you are angry! It is the quickest way to get a lump in your throat.
(8) If you pay bills online, have everything with you when you begin paying them. Checkbook, credit cards, account numbers, etc. If you pay in person, only take the bill you are "actually" going to pay.
(9) If you pay online, keep confirmation numbers relating to the payment. If you pay in person, keep your receipt in a receipt envelope.

JUST LET GO!

These suggestions will help alleviate carrying around unnecessary stress. Stop dragging bills and other documents around with you that should be kept in a safe place. Remember, sensitive data is on your bills. Don't carry anything that should be stored in a designated place. "JUST LET GO" of this and other bad habits that can cause negative tension to be harbored throughout your life!

JUST LET GO OF THE REMOTE
Too Much T.V.

Here is another "bad habit" that we all can "Just Let Go" of, if we are addicted! You might not realize it, but aimlessly sitting in front of a T.V. every day is really not good for you. The thought is that you are watching T.V., but in the 21st century with satellites beaming in on our car tags from outer space, the question should be, is "T.V." actually watching you. The smart T.V.'s are capable of watching "you!" Want to feel 10 lbs. lighter? Then dump something that makes you feel bad, regardless of what it is. In this world, our young and old alike are systematically being entertained by a tube of people who are making money every minute we stay tuned to a channel they are on. In turn, you are paying the station and the celebrity's bills simultaneously as we scramble our brains leaving our bills unpaid. Even while you sit there watching the tube, your brain is actually on "mute!" The brain mutes itself when it is not actively processing something worthwhile that is coming from you. It's called "mental time out."

Think about this for a moment. The next time you want to watch Life Time Movies all day…count how many stories you will watch before your brain goes "numb!" It really gets to you after a while viewing the same scenarios over and over again. Just new character's needing to make a pay check. So instead of the tube, why not "READ A BOOK!" Find one that would be exciting for you and a good, clean easy read. If you are addicted to the tube and want to correct this? "JUST LET GO OF THE REMOTE!" Put it in the garage with the mail you don't want to open… ☺

JUST LET GO!

JUST LET GO
of
Fear

Now the topics are becoming more intense! Let's discuss something we all have experienced in life. "FEAR!" Fear can be a spooky word. It is also a "learned" behavior and based on a psychological term called "classical conditioning." It is sometimes developed through our environment and other factors which may cause us to be afraid of things or people. Fear is not all bad either. Some people may like a little "spooky" movie where you become a bit agitated in a good way. It gets the adrenaline going and it feels good. The old horror flicks that people use to watch was just the ticket for that Saturday night excitement before bed! The other type of fear is that which causes the "fight-or-flight syndrome which is "not" so good. It prompts our mind and body to react to saving itself when there is no imminent danger. When people have panic attacks, this process takes effect.

As mentioned, all fear is not bad. In the instance of a person standing on a railroad track and hears a train whistle blow. The hair may stand up on their neck which tells them, they need to get off the tracks as soon as possible, but they still must determine, which track? That fear doesn't leave until you are out of harm's way. It also gives you the needed adrenaline rush to help you make that decision to run, scurry or do whatever it takes to be safe again. This type of fear helps you deal with things that are short term. Animals also have a similar type of fear. It's called "instinct." Bad fear is sometimes based on the "what if'" factors in life. No one can tell the future, but if we could, there would be no need to fear at all. The bad fear causes the same reactions as the good fear, but without the lasting actuality of something taking place at that moment.

JUST LET GO!

If bad fear was constant, we would never want to go outside, or go to a park for fear that someone there might start randomly shooting. Or, no one would ever board a plane believing that "all" planes will crash just because. Because what? That should be the question when you want to squelch your fears! Some people have been afraid to drive on the highway because there are eighteen wheelers on the road. Now, that's serious, but true! Remember, when certain fears appear, our bodies go into the fight or flight mode. You have shortness of breath, sweaty palms, increased heart rate, but there is no danger, only "perceived" danger. But when we watch a Sci-fi movie, we have increased heart rate, shortness of breath at certain scenes, but we know we are watching a movie in the safety of our home so the feeling will soon go away. So, why do so many people have extreme amounts of bad fear?

Some of it is learned from childhood. Some is from current personal situations or having been frightened by someone or something. Sometimes it is due to adult experiences of being in the War and suffering from PTSD. However, long term fear can weigh you down and prevent you from using your mental faculties to the full. We are slow to move forward with bad fears if they are out of control. Bad fears imprison us and keeps us from making changes in our lives that hinder positive growth. Bad fear can become a ball and chain in our lives when we wear it daily. Over time, we may refuse to try anything new for "fear" we will fare badly. Sometimes people don't want to change because it requires making adjustments to themselves that can be difficult. But the truth of the matter is that everything around us is changing and holding onto the way things were yesterday can cripple us "tomorrow."

 **Just Let GO**

www.victoriaekain.com

JUST LET GO!

What if people born in the 40's chose never to use a telephone in 2016? They probably would never go anywhere alone. Sometimes, we must embrace change in our lives whether we want to or not. Being willing to be knowledgeable of the change taking place and keeping ourselves abreast of it is a good thing! We must accept how we personally benefit from change as opposed to panicking about it. Once you embrace it, you can remove most bad fear of the unknown. Most of us are comfortable with things we "know," and don't venture too far from that because it takes a lot of "courage" to do so. How we embrace the unknown will determine how successful we are with making changes. What's the best way to begin accepting change? Let's see the suggestions below and see how our lives might change with a clearer view.

WHEN MAKING CHANGE...BE SPECIFIC ABOUT WHAT YOU WANT TO DO!

Scenario: If you are someone who has never travelled much in your lifetime because of living in remote areas where walking was the mode of travel, how would you accept that you now must use another way to travel? First, you might consider which mode of transportation you might prefer knowing the old way is no longer an option. Trains, or Planes? Pick your poison! Because the railways came about first, you think about what you've heard from those who have already taken their first train ride. You glean information from the positive and negative stories you were told and usually weigh out which served you best in the way the stories ended. You might express in a casual conversation with someone close that you might like to take a train ride instead of a plane. Talking about the change you are about to make helps ease your mind about doing something completely different.

You determined that your fear of heights completely remove you from accepting the travel arrangements by plane and you quickly dispel that fear which makes you focus more on the only other choice available. Now with the decision made to travel by train, you gather as much information as possible to help remove any final fears about this mode of travel.

JUST LET GO!

With weeks left to go before you take that first ride, your brain is in full gear about the massive vehicle you will ride. At some point late in the evening, you may begin to feel a few butterflies in the pit of your stomach. This is from the unknown of an event that has not taken place yet. Still, you force yourself to move forward and try not to talk yourself out of doing what you must do.

Days go by and you remember that "fear" is created when there is the "unknown." Once you try something, you have broken the ice of whatever it is you are doing for the first time but in order not to drop back into the fear mode, you must keep making "change." Making change, makes sense. Finally the day comes and you board the train. You sit quietly and your brain recalls all the things you have heard from those who have taken the mammoth ride. You look around your cabin watching people chatter aimlessly as if everything is normal. You want to fit in so you abruptly strike up a conversation with your traveling companion which calms you down.

In this instance, you get through the trip with flying colors. You depart the train with your chest out looking around at all the passengers scurrying by as if they had just finished walking from somewhere. A little nervousness hits you as you look back at the train slowly moving out of the gate. You watch the people in the windows looking out and you wonder if one of them is taking their first trip as you just did. This scenario was simple in that doing something we haven't done before can be challenging when you become overly concerned about the minor things. This is when anxiety and fear may creep in.

Even still, try not to focus on negative things when you are doing something for the first time. Unless there is a true reason to be concerned, "don't!" Don't think about the speed of the train, or how high up the plane is if you are flying. If you are claustrophobic about flying, don't remind yourself that you can't get off the plane for two hours. Doing so could send you into a panic attack so think about something else. Try to read a book or listen to music. Don't get a window seat if you don't like to fly. People who love to fly always want to sit by the window and will trade seats for the view.

JUST LET GO!

They love seeing the clouds below them. Others, who hate flying but will board a plane to get somewhere fast, do not want to gaze at the wing of the plane. The biggest issue for most people on flying is that they hate not being able to see the ground. The truth of the matter is that it is probably safer in the air than it is on the ground these days, yet millions of people fly every day and think nothing of it. I often said that my sister would get on anything with a wing or feathers that could lift itself off the ground even if it had feet because she loved travelling all over the world. I only wish I had her guts for flying. It's not that I don't trust the planes, it's the pilots I'm most concerned about! If all else fails to calm your nerves of fear on a flight, watch the stewardesses. They value their lives the same as anyone else, so why would they take a job believing that as soon as they take off for work on a flight the plane will crash! Exactly!!! They did their homework on the safety record of travelling by plane and as mentioned, it's safer in the air than on the ground!

So when it's time to make changes in your life and you become fearful, think positive! Once you take that first step forward to do something different like changing your mode of travel…don't look back! After you do whatever it is, give yourself as many positives as you can to flood your brain with stored data about the change you just made and squelch any fear you had. Do something memorable so that you have more positive things to recall. This will help remove the fear. Say these positive things. "That wasn't so bad after all!" Or, I really liked the friendliness of the crew! "It was a great flight!" Soon you will pay little attention to it and arrive at your destination safely.

The best suggestion is to take short trips on either non-stop flights if you don't like changing planes. Or, if you prefer to break up the travel, take one with a short layover where it brings you down out of the sky which satisfies the claustrophobic issue. This works very well if you have the time to do it. Keep graduating to the next change. It is that simple! It doesn't mean that if you prefer the "train" you can't favor that mode of travel, but allow yourself to have options.

JUST LET GO!

Learn how to take the "fear" out of living. It doesn't mean being reckless... just live! Be clear about your desires because it helps you embrace awareness. Identify your feelings and thoughts and examine the beliefs you may have learned over time which could make you fearful for no reason. Remember, if something doesn't fit, then don't force it regardless of what it is. Also, give your fears a name. Calling it what you want it to be can sometimes make it less intimidating. Focus on what you can do about your bad fears and utilize your mental and physical energy to draw your thoughts away from them. Be aware of what prevents you from changing. Say "No" to unsupported bad fears and only accept those that actually serve a purpose in your life.

"Change is Good When it Makes Sense"

Whoever threw away a pocket full of loose "change?" Exactly! Once we realize that "change" is not our enemy, we can move forward. We begin by taking the first steps to conquering our bad fears and we are clear on what we need to do with them. We should focus on our new awareness of where these fears originate from and then make the necessary adjustment to discard them and it makes sense to do so. Consider this as a final point. When we grow up with certain negative beliefs, we nurture "bad fear." An example of this would be: fear of walking under a ladder. Fear of a black cat crossing our path. Fear of breaking a mirror. Washing clothes on Sunday. Crossing your eyes or legs at a certain time or fearing Friday the 13th. It's just another day in the week. These are only a few things that may cause us to hold on to bad fear. Yet many people today believe in these superstitions and live by them which cripples their lives. Some individuals learned fears from childhood. They heard frightening stories about things that no longer happen. For now, we should view our fears as REAL. While some good fears keep you safe by causing you to react in an emergency, some bad fears can cause you to create an emergency! Be open to new things and rid yourself of bad fear that prohibits you from being at your best game to "Just let Go," of anything that does not fit where you are in your life today!

JUST LET GO!

JUST LET GO!
ANGER/FRUSTRATION

Anger is another powerful emotion that can be confusing. When anger appears, it usually intensifies matters and makes things worse. Most people try to avoid becoming angry, but sadly, being imperfect causes most of us to fail that task miserably! Why do humans get angry? Why do these emotions exist? Anger gets out of hand for a million reasons depending on what is said or done. Unlike the animals, why don't we have more control as humans? If animals became as angry as humans do over insignificant things, there would be chaos in the jungle. Each person handles anger differently, but why? How can we control this two edged sword. When we can understand this emotion in its various forms, we can assess how to combat it. There are different techniques to handle someone who has annoyed you, or have actually caused you to become angry.

Anger is an emotion which serves as an interim reaction to something or someone that "threatens" us or our love ones. Anger lets humans know that something is wrong and it lets people know that you are dissatisfied with something. There are several facets of anger. How you address your anger makes the difference between a positive or negative outcome.

JUST LET GO!

It is the physical reaction to anger that lets you know that a "threat" is ensuing. This is when the "fight or flight" response kicks in. The cognitive part of that is how we view anger and why things make us angry. An example could be… we may feel that our mate broke up with us for something stupid and it wasn't fair. We simply didn't deserve it. Feasibly we could be angry and maybe cry all night brooding over the incident or we could take a brick and break out all the windows in the individuals SUV. Don't try this at home.

That would be the difference in how the person perceived what made them angry and their rationale about it. Have no fear though, anger is a normal emotion. The dictionary defines it as many things which include, a strong feeling of displeasure, hostility, rage, vexation exasperation, crossness, irritation, irritability, indignation, annoyance, fury, wrath, outrage. These are some of the types of anger and most of these are predicated on what the person had for breakfast that morning. Adults and children become angry for similar reason. When we do not get the things we want, many people become "angry" with the individuals or other entities that prevent them from acquiring what they want or need. A child is the same.

They become angry and exhibit their anger by crying when they don't get something they want. Adults may sulk or even argue about what they want and sometimes may resort to the infantile crying to have their way. Anger is usually provoked by someone or something in our lives. Sometimes people are rightfully angry about things done to them or their loved ones that they may not be able to let go of. There is a down fall to this train of thought. Anger is real, and it can be dangerous when it is harbored. When a wrong has been committed against an innocent person, this is usually painful. It is natural to be angry trying to figure out "why" someone would harm someone else for no reason. However, when the pain can never take its proper place in our lives it gives birth to brooding which in the long term can cause physical and mental health issues.

JUST LET GO!

There must be some form of emotional release in order to eliminate stress that has been inherited here, otherwise the brooding can continue to pop up like summer thunder showers and can range from mild to severe. When this happens it can control our thoughts and actions which could become violent or uncontrolled. In this instance of anger remember that there are dangers to holding onto anger. It can create a vicious cycle and we become its prisoner. Depression is another part of what anger turns into if not controlled over time. We may not want to harm anyone else, but may turn to drugs, alcohol or other self-abuses. Eating disorders have also been linked to this type of reaction. Some individuals who allow their anger to go from brooding to rumination can make poor decisions about their health choices to build up their cardio vascular routines to promote good health.

But, how can we Let Go when things hurt us? Identify why you are angry. Ask yourself if you can fix it, remove it, or cure it? If you can't do either of those things, you must learn to "LET IT GO!" Remember that when we make mistakes, it is an opportunity to learn. Even with the mistakes we make, if it's still difficult to let go of anger, try setting aside a time to ponder over what could be the source of our anger. That's right, the same as you would set aside time to take a lunch break at work, set a time aside to "ponder over why you are angry," but don't give it a whole hour. Set your timer and give yourself no more than 10 full minutes. Once you finish worrying your head off for that 10 minutes as to why you are angry, if you can't come up with a logical reason, you must move on to the day. However, you can only ponder over this for 10 minutes, each day…You get the idea! Eventually when you see your time being wasted over spending 10 minutes trying to be angry about something you can't come up with, you will push the time further and further apart and eventually realize there was nothing that important to cause you to be that angry in the first place.

Just Let GO

Victoria E. Kain

JUST LET GO!

Soon you will no longer have the need to worry about the "thing" that had encompassed your life and made you think you were angry. Also, exercise is an excellent therapy. If that doesn't work see a therapist to help you sort out fears, anger, and anxiety. Either way, face your anger and fears head on. At some phase of life, you should begin to see that life is an action word. In order to get the most out of it, you must be "LIVING." The world has enough super heroes, so "Just Let Go" of anger and live without fear or anxiety!

JUST LET GO
of
Jealousy

Jealousy has been deemed the "green eyed monster," in the mythical books of old. That green with envy attitude was attached to people that were jealous and they were usually deemed "evil" as well. Among those were the wicked step mother in Cinderella, the wicked witch of the west in the Wizard of Oz and who could forget Cruella De'vil the hater of those beautiful spotted pups! These were the villains of the stories who always got what they deserved in the end. They were jealous of someone or of something that someone else had that they wanted. They begrudged the good guy or girl for helping others in a time of need. The jealous ones didn't care who got hurt, they wanted to destroy them! However, that is what happens in the movies, but jealousy today has taken a turn for the worse. In past years, it has gone from a harmless school girl crush on a boy that took another girl to the prom and the girl that was not asked, cried herself to sleep that night. Today, that story ends with the jilted girl murdering the boy and the girl that went to the prom together and the event was posted on Face book or YouTube making the six o'clock news. All because of jealousy! What ever happened to getting another date???

JUST LET GO!

Would it really be necessary to turn into "Carrie?" Knives slinging from one end of the room to the next??? People's emotions and their environments have a lot to do with how they cope with their situations and jealousy and peer pressure is deadly for today's teens and young adults. Many programs on television show young people in very stressful situations competing against their peers for titles or money and the world at large votes for them. This is a dangerous position for most youths to be in if they are not grounded. Some youths and adults look to these venues as a way to validate themselves. The judges are very direct and the viewers are critical and can tell that the young singers or dancers are crushed when they are booted off the show once they are no longer a contender to be sent to the infamous city of "HOLLYWOOD!"

Really!!! It is sad when the youths get a small taste of what it's like to be a "STAR," and then have to say goodbye as they fall back to earth in the blink of an eye. Their lives could have been changed forever! It would be interesting to see the shows based on what happens to the people that don't make it in these contests. We know that many are emotionally crippled for life and feel like a failure for no reason. They simply had not yet learned how to look at the positives from where they were at the moment. You never hear from some of them again. It's like the let-down never lets up! Jealousy has become rampant within our society, but why do people become jealous of someone else in the first place?

The reasons are as numerous as the grains of sand are on a beach in Hawaii and may depend on who the jealousy is directed towards. If you are jealous, what does the person mean to you that you are jealous of? What do they have that you wish you had? Do they have more friends? Longer legs, smoother skin, less zits, longer hair, curly eye lashes? The ability to get the things they want? Who knows? Since we are speaking on jealousies, let's look at one scenario dealing with relationships. This could be a real or imagined issue. It could be, a younger woman married to an older man. In this case, the younger woman may be jealous of "ANYONE" if the special attention from her older spouse is not there. Also, if there is money involved.

JUST LET GO!

The jealousy could stem from the older man being very generous to the younger woman's friends. But, this may not be the reason for the jealousy. The jealousy might come from the older spouse not giving his younger spouse his undivided attention. The younger woman may become jealous when her older spouse gives special attention to her friends or even his friends and family. The jealousy is being fueled because something is lacking in the relationship. What is it? The special attention from her older spouse. The woman soon feels "she" is not being given the just due of her older mate's attention and may begin to feel sad when attention is shown to others and not her. She may feel that she landed the "catch" of the day and no one else should feast off the spoils but her. While we understand those feelings, it also depends on many other factors as well.

The younger woman may not make many waves depending on how wealthy the older spouse is, realizing that the older spouse may not choose to tolerate much of the outward jealousy, so the younger woman may choose to seethe in silence and jealousies can grow fast undercover. She may not attack the older mate, but will let the women know they are receiving what she feels is rightfully "hers! These are common reactions in situations of older/younger relationships of men and women. Yet, the jealousy can be rectified if the person who is jealous realizes that they "are" receiving what they want from the older mate and there is no true threat to the relationship. Jealousy becomes more of a vindictive situation when one person becomes obsessed with seeing others being treated nice. There still must be a balance to this generosity in the case of this younger woman and older man, but still the younger woman should be able to hold her own without becoming incensed and allowing jealousy to take over and potentially destroy a good relationship. Now let's reverse the situation! It is the same with jealousy from an older "man" younger woman when the older man is jealous. Sometimes just having a younger woman as a mate who does nice things to help other couples can make some men insanely jealous.

JUST LET GO!

For men jealousy may go a little deeper even in cases where there is nothing going on at all. When an older man is jealous of his younger partner, the jealousy could come from being insecure where other younger "men" are concerned. The older man may feel that his younger female partner may be receiving more attention from other men which could make him jealous. The older man may not want his younger partner to even "smile" as they always do because of a haywire jealous streak. Sometimes jealousy can cause an older man to refrain from taking his younger female partner out in public where other males might frequent. Especially if she is pretty. This gets old very quickly!

It can be dangerous if it gets out of control. It's like the beautiful princess being locked away in the Kings castle, and eventually, "Rapunzel" will let down her golden hair for the young prince! Remember, jealousy comes in many forms. It can be seen in families with sibling rivalry, parents, work mates, clergy, you name it. The simple fact is this: Jealousy is a form of coveting. Wanting something or begrudging someone for what they have. So how can the older man younger woman couple solve their issue? In this instance, the couple could consider discussing their likes and dislikes of habits they both may have when entertaining other people's attention towards them.

There may be no reason in the world to be jealous, but some people can't seem to stop it! One way to curtail feelings such as these is to realize that if someone has something you like, and you begin to envision it being yours....buy one of your own if there's more of them! If they have the only one of its kind, ask them if they would like to "sell" it to you. If it's their eyes, hair, DNA or something they were born with...just walk away! Don't resolve that you would rather see them D-E-A-D if you can't have what belongs to them. Remember that everything has a price, but some things are price LESS and irreplaceable! Do you want to pay the price for taking something that is not rightfully yours? If you do, remember...there is a stiff penalty involved! If not, respect that being "jealous" about it or them is not going to solve the issue.

JUST LET GO!

Even the worse decisions we make when we take jealous emotions to the extreme will cost us more than we are physically and mentally prepared to pay. When jealousy is out of control, it becomes "rage." Rage can destroy lives. If you find yourself feeling "that" jealous about anything, ask yourself why you are feeling that way! Then analyze it. Squash the thought quickly before it gives birth to "jealous rage." Remember that Jealousy has the word "LOUSY" in it! You will feel "lousy" when you covet what others have and it's difficult to let go of those types of feelings. They burrow into our subconscious and eats away at our very core. Realize that in life, we only need a few things to be happy. One of those things is "peace of mind!" When we get "some" of the things we really want in life, nothing else should matter. Our sanity and living a happy life should be on the front burner of our hearts. If you are jealous, you could find yourself in deep water without a life jacket and robbing yourself of all the beautiful things on the shores of life! So, be happy with what you have and live life to the full! Let go of petty jealousies and be happy!

"JUST LET GO OF GUILT"

Guilty or Not Guilty?

Guilt comes in many forms and may take on many different facets in our lives. It is an emotion that appears when someone believes they have compromised themselves in some way. When moral standards are violated, many people feel a sense of "guilt." They may feel that they are legally responsible for what may have occurred due to their violating an action they should have performed to right a wrong. When you have remorse or regret for doing something or not, and feeling a sense of obligation, that is a form of "guilt." Many of us carry around "unnecessary" guilt about things that weigh us down. Here is a simple example of subliminal "guilt" we might carry around unnecessarily.

JUST LET GO!

"PARENTAL GUILT"

In this example, we discuss parents and their unfounded feelings of guilt with their children. *Imagine a cuddly, lovable baby, adored by parents, grandparents, family and friends. When the child demands anything, he receives it with love and can get it from everyone in the family. Soon the child becomes a toddler and grows up healthy. They are lovingly trained by the parents to take their first steps. Then second and third steps and now the child can run to each parent with minimal assistance. Time pass and the loving parents take their child, now 3 years old, on their first big outing to an amusement park. The first inclination is for the parents to carry the child and whisper things in its ear about their new surroundings.*

The parent might even resort to carrying the child for a time because of the crowds. Soon the child is getting heavy and the parent begins shifting the baby from arm to arm trying to relieve some of the pressure being put on their own bodies from carrying the extra weight. If the mother is carrying the child, she might subliminally reason that she "carried" the child in the womb, so why not now...after all, it's "her" baby. Thereby taking the responsibility for the baby's comfort and her seeming responsibility to continue "carrying" the child through the crowded park. That thought process feels good for a while until the mother's arms become red and sore and now partially numb from carrying the child for so long. She continues to carry him out of unfounded obligation but is now becoming exhausted and agitated. Feeling guilty about wanting to put him down and obligated to make him comfortable, she finally must re-think the situation.

JUST LET GO!

She quickly retracts her initial thoughts about the obvious realizing that the child will always be her child, but in the womb, he was only 5lbs 6oz and not the 27 pounds he is now. The mother quickly reasoned that the child "can" walk for short stents of time. In this instance the mother is now re-conditioning her "emotions" which is the first step to removing guilt in any situation. She then, began removing the "guilt" feeling of not being a good parent because she wanted to make herself comfortable by allowing the child to walk for a spell even though there would be no discomfort to the child. Guilt is an amazing emotion because in order to let it go, you must reason honestly from the heart and use facts that are acceptable. She then gave her heart permission to tell her brain that it was okay to be "relieved" from carrying the baby's additional weight. Lastly, to ensure that the baby did not feel rejected, the parent preps the child by telling them they will put them down to walk for a while. This conditions the child's mental state to accept the fact that they will now walk for a while. The parent puts the child down and lovingly hold their hand. The mother is instantly relieved of her physical and mental pain of carrying the extra weight and her guilt was also removed.

How often have we accused and convicted ourselves of something that "NOONE" charged us with? There was no evidence, no eye witnesses or any proof that we were "guilty" of anything. Yet, we beat ourselves into the ground feeling bad about something that we either had no control over or really had nothing to do with it in the first place.

In this scenario, we have just witnessed a self-inflicted "guilt." Many times "we" convict ourselves of things no one has charged us with. In this instance the parent wanted to believe they would be negligent if they didn't carry their child around even though they could walk. Her thinking had to be adjusted to resolve the unfounded guilt. We must re-vamp our "thinking" from time to time and bring it in line with what is reasonable. But we must remember that if we are carrying guilt that is unfounded, we must bring all aspects of the matter to our mental "court" and examine it thoroughly.

Then, we must accept the decision we have rendered to ourselves and acquit our own conscious of any wrong doing and be "guilt free."

JUST LET GO!

The point is "don't" carry around anything or anyone that is able to carry its own weight! This mindset of harboring unfounded guilt has hindered many!" Loving someone or something doesn't mean that you cannot let it go if the time is right. So...if you have guilt feelings, examine the issue thoroughly and render a decision. Free yourself from the drudgery of hauling negative feelings around unnecessarily like the 27 pound baby being carried too long. Know when to let go of guilt. Even in instances where a person may take "responsibility" for something, there are still ways to reason logically as to why what was done was or was not necessary. Give yourself options to rule everything out before condemning yourself or others. Remember that removing any "negative" thoughts from our minds is a "positive" action and well worth the effort. Stop feeling that you must do "everything" for family, children, spouses, bosses, or others even when they can do it for themselves. When you do things for people that they can clearly do for themselves, it could indicate that you receive some intrinsic reward for putting yourself in this position. If this is the case, there are many who would love to have you around and would gladly "pay" you for your services of cleaning, doing laundry and watching their kids. When you learn this, you will feel much better about you and your relationship with your child. Learning how, when and why to let go of any extra weight as a parent is vitally important to your child's future mental and physical growth. This positive change in attitude can help guide us in many ways. We must find ways to see how this concept of letting go might work where we feel guilty about things that may not even exist at all. "Just Let Go!"

"LET GO OF BEING A VICTIM!"

Victimization is real! It is also a touchy subject. There are millions of people who have been "victimized" at one time or another in their lives. Every year, thousands of people are taken advantage of by a family member, spouse, close friend, trusted official, clergy, stranger or other. Many of these perpetrators go unscathed by the authorities for various reasons leaving a rubble of their victim's lives hanging in the balance trying to live a normal life in a twisted society.

JUST LET GO!

Many have sat in the victims' seat not knowing how they will survive the aftermath of trying to let go of the pain forever. When humans are violated, they find themselves in the precarious position of housing natural emotions in an unnatural setting. There is fear, anger, love, hatred, empathy and indifference. In many instances, some or all of these emotions can manifest themselves at the same time. It doesn't matter the gender, they all have the same reaction to being taken advantage of. Pain and suffering becomes their new enemy and their "brain" becomes the new battle ground.

In this instance, the "brain" takes on its own entity and becomes the "new" victimizer. Pain will be the accomplice when the incident is remembered and will cause the victim to become restless, angry, silent or even violent at inopportune times. It will rob its prey of sleep and happiness over and over again as they try to figure out a solution to stop the barrage of "thoughts" that flood their memory. How can people cope with the invisible thing they cannot control? How do they remove the fear of having to constantly embrace the unwanted pain they now must nurture like an infant child feeding from its mother? This scenario is a true story of a young woman who "Beat" victimization from her childhood. Once she realized how badly she was handling her personal life after the incident many years earlier, she leaped into action to protect the ones she loved. Her negative past was clouding the happiness she could see far off in her distant future. See how this woman fought to change a negative behavior and mindset in order to let go of her past.

We understand that there is no perfect cure for any ailment that plagues mankind. Yet, we continue to strive to find ways to rid ourselves of what ails us. In a world inundated with medications and other such treatments, if we can work through a process without the aid of medication, shock treatments or other harmful procedures, we may be able to heal as we go along without major side effects. However, we need a strong support system. Peggy took steps to begin the process of analyzing her mental state of being a victim. It's time to meet "Peggy."

JUST LET GO!

"A Positive Approach to Life!"

A young girl named "Peggy" lived with her family. Her mother was a homemaker and occasionally took college classes to better herself. Her father worked on the railroad and was hardly home but provided well for them even though they were not rich, they had everything they needed. Peggy felt she had a good life like all the other kids she knew. Being an only child, she didn't want for much and was always brought pretty things when her father would return home from being gone sometimes for months.

When her father came home from his trips, he had all kinds of great stories to tell Peggy and her mother about his travels and they would sit and listen intently as they both were always glad to see him when he returned. Soon Peggy's father would receive awards for the work he did on the railroad. He received high commendations and promotions which made him very important and respected by his superiors. Because of this, he would be gone even longer times now and Peggy and her mother felt alone.

Life went on for Peggy and her mother and soon they would get the notification from her father when he would be arriving home. They hurried to make the house ready and prepared a big meal. They knew he would have great stories and gifts for them both and merrily went about their chores. Soon the moment came and Peggy's father was at the door! They gave the traditional hugs and later sat down to have dinner.

The stories were told as usual, but Peggy noticed that her father was different when he came home this time. Even though she was young, she noticed that he seemed to pay a different type of attention to her which did not concern her much but she knew it was different. They finished their evening and since her father would be home for weeks this time, she would have lots of time with him. Peggy's mother had taken a class in the city and would leave in the evening for about three hours or so. Tonight, Peggy had planned to watch a movie with her father that evening and soon he would prepare the popcorn.

JUST LET GO!

Her father soon came into the living room where she sat on the sofa anticipating his arrival. The popcorn was on the coffee table as well. Her father came in and sat next to her, but she noticed that he smelled of alcohol this time. This was unusual for Peggy because she didn't know that he drank. She soon tried to push the thought away and focused on the movie. As her father sat next to her, he became more focused on her in a way that was uncomfortable. He tried to be playful in his touch but Peggy became uncomfortable to the point that she went to her room and locked the door. Confused as to the change in her father's behavior, she didn't know if she should tell her mother. Sadly, she chose not to say anything. Her father left after that week and this time, she didn't think as much about him being gone as she had in the past.

Her mind was preoccupied with why he had touched her the way he had which was not normal. Still being her father, she loved him but didn't understand because she was so young. The weeks went by fast and then it was time for her father to come home again. This time, she was not as chipper about his arrival because she didn't know what to expect. Her mother was still in school so she asked in advance if she could go with her, but her mother told her no, that she could spend that time with her father.

Once home, her father acted as if nothing had happened on his last visit. She soon thought it was all in her head since she had no physical pain or scars. Her mother went to class as usual and soon her father asked if she wanted to watch a movie with him. He made the same popcorn. She declined and said she wanted to play with her dolls and was ever so polite about refusing the personal time with him. She went in her room and closed her door. She could hear the television and fell sound asleep. Soon, Peggy was awakened by her father kneeling beside her bed. She was partially unclothed and now was afraid. Her father quickly left the room swearing her to secrecy and it was not discussed again. Peggy's father left to go back on the train early that week. It was as if he didn't want to face her mother for fear she would suspect something. This was the beginning of Peggy's victimization.

JUST LET GO!

Being so young at the onset of these encounters, Peggy did not understand what was happening or why. When there is no lasting physical pain or scars when something happens to children, it may be difficult to detect by a parent or caregiver. The child may simply brush it off until something hurts them to the point that it is noticeable. For Peggy, she endured these occasional encounters with her father for sporadic periods of time. She never told anyone believing she was protecting the family she loved. Time flew by and she was in Middle school. Her father would stay gone longer after each encounter which put a strain on her parents' marriage. Soon, her parents divorced. It was a difficult change in her life, but she felt she was finally free thinking that everything would be better for her now. She no longer feared the late night visits but still felt the void of not having a father at home.

Time moved by swiftly and Peggy finished high school. Instinctively, she looked for her father in the audience at her graduation, but tossed the thought out, wondering why she even bothered to think it in the first place after what he had done to her as a child. She quickly moved past that part of her life and thought it was over. However, when we mature and are old enough to understand when something has happened to us as a child, our brain goes to work and we soon will give it all the "overtime" it needs to "recreate" some of the incidents in our lives in order to answer the questions only the "perpetrator" can answer...yet our brain keeps trying to answer them to no avail.

Peggy was full grown now and noticed that she had begun to daydream about some of the encounters from her past. At some moments, she mentally focused on recreating the incidents and it felt like something ghostly taking over her body with physical and mental emotions. It's not what she wanted to do, it just seemed to manifest itself at inopportune times. It was many years before she was completely clear as to why she had certain feelings about certain things. While she was at home with her mother, it was different with the day dreams and night sweats.

JUST LET GO!

After Peggy married and had children of her own, she was soon thrust head first into her past as a realization of what she had experienced and how it was affecting her life and the lives of those she loved. She was now faced with the brutal task of unloading all of the guilt, pain, fear, and unrealistic expectations on those around her, and she executed the command subconsciously. Now the victimization effect was in full bloom staring her straight in the face. She realized that what she saw happening in her life with her family, was being fueled by what had happened to her as a child. Then the pain truly began. Peggy later realized many of her issues came from the early abuse.

Scores of people go for years beating themselves up about what happened to them in their past and may find themselves beating others down in order to fight the effects of various abuses. *Years went by and Peggy began realizing certain behavioral changes that had manifested in her life. She determined that she would beat this demon and would not hand these feelings down to another generation. She learned to listen to the things she thought and think about what she told herself.*

In order to clear her conscience of any guilt feelings, she finally told her mother what had happened to her. Her mother was devastated but told her daughter she would help her fight the demon. After much deliberation, Peggy purged herself of everything that happened and day after day they dissected the information piece by piece. Then Peggy made a list of the things she ruminated over throughout the day. She listed habits she had developed and then analyzed those. She wondered why she was afraid of the dark and didn't understand it. When her children were born, she loved them dearly but had this fetish about "them" being in the dark. She insisted on putting night lights in her children's rooms so they wouldn't be afraid. While this is something most parents do anyway, she later realized after an honest assessment of her motives, that "she" was the one that needed the night lights.

JUST LET GO!

She remembered the dark encounters that made her nervous when she went to bed as a child and now understood why she feared the dark and feared it for her children. For that reason, she kept a "light" in the children's room to illuminate it so "they" could see if anyone would ever come to their room. When she realized why she needed the nightlight, she cried but these were tears of joy! She was finally free of this behavior that was in place which masked her fear from childhood. It was further understood that by assessing that this was for the "children" she was negating that "she" had been abused at all.

Soon, Peggy dissected each negative behavior, one by one the same way. She addressed problems with walking past patio doors at night if the curtains were half drawn. She realized it was the subliminal fear that the perpetrator might be lurking outside waiting to attack her again, yet he was nowhere to be found. The young woman unknowingly had found ways to keep the perpetrator alive in her mind by "thinking" about him. It was like a fire you make in the forest. If you continue to feed the fire with something it will keep burning for a long time. But if you want to put the fire "out" you stop "feeding" it and it soon will die out. Peggy was putting out many fires!

She remembered going through a phase of hating the color "pink." It was not that anything was wrong with the color, but to her, she stated that it represented something "frilly, or girl like" which represented "vulnerability." The feeling was that if she had not been "vulnerable" she would not have been taken advantage of and would have fought back. In order to let go of this issue, she had to remind herself that she was only six years old when the incidents began to occur. She was not able to fight back. She was a child and children are sometimes "vulnerable" to individuals and things that are "bigger" than they are. She blamed herself for what happened which is common, but this is what causes the "victim" syndrome.

JUST LET GO!

Then, Peggy addressed why she never wanted to smile. Or, why she was obsessed with cleaning. She hated using terms such as "panties" which again represented a female, and chose to use non-gender specific terms such as, "underwear." When she referenced her children's clothing, she didn't want them to wear anything that appeared revealing. She would layer her clothes and the children's until they were old enough to dress themselves. She felt that layering protected them as it would have protected her during the incidents as a child. She hated seeing "stains" on clothing because it represented something unclean. For a short period, any "stained" clothing, her children had were thrown away. She did this until her budget dictated that she stop! Her mind had taken over and now she understood what happened to her and saw how her anger was being feed as she tried to fight the invisible foe.

She wanted to do something to change the horrible habits she had nurtured. Soon the fetish of leaving dishes in the sink would be no more. For years the woman weathered the storm of the aftermath of being abused and being mentally victimized long after the abuse was over. She realized that each time she allowed her brain to take over, she victimized herself by "ruminating" and reliving the horrible feelings she experienced over and over again. "Why me?" Was always the question. The young woman lived a life that almost crippled her. When we get to the point where we feel we are no longer living for ourselves but for an entity that has taken over our minds and for some…their bodies, we must find someone else to live for until we can see ourselves as being worthy enough to find our way back to our reality.

Through the help of God and her family, she stated that while the thoughts are sometimes there, they no longer cripple her existence. She decided that she had to give more of herself to her husband and children in order to free herself from the guilt that had been heaped upon her from the rubble of her sordid life.

JUST LET GO!

Peggy was determined that she would work towards unraveling the negative behaviors she had inadvertently developed from the sexual encounters many years earlier. When asked what helped her in this process, she stated, "writing down some of the impulsive behaviors after an episode helped and then one by one I would tackle them."

Soon her obsession with a dish being left in the sink which was related to something "dirty" was minimized by consciously leaving one dish in the sink "each night." When she would look at the dish she would recondition her brain to accept that the "dish" had nothing to do with what had happened in her life. The dish was the "trigger" for her brain to dredge up bad memories to keep her feeling worthless. She ultimately was able to work through the obsession realizing that the "dish" became an extension to fuel her "pain" of not being able to reverse the negative experience. She also concluded over time that she did not have to come "unglued" if there was anything in the sink anymore.

Slowly she stopped using dirty dishes as what she considered as a representation of how she felt on the inside. Cleaning the "dirty" dishes made her feel as if she had "hidden" what happened to her and no one would think ill of her. Until then, she did not realize that no one ever would have thought that she was "dirty" in the first place. She was "innocent." Soon Peggy no longer had to hide her feelings because she was not a child, but an adult who had "all" the control she needed to protect herself and her family.

Recognizing that "she" was in control, helped her refute the negative thoughts that took "control" of her in the past! This was part of the internal victimization being removed from her psyche. She could now live her life the way she wanted to live it.

JUST LET GO!

Over time, Peggy was freed of "guilt" feelings blaming herself for things she was "not" responsible for. Her relationship with her mother was very strong and she never blamed her for not knowing. She loved her even more for helping her work through her potentially dangerous situation. Peggy is still happily married and lives comfortably with her family. She treasures having the ability to work through her issues and wants to share this with the world. End.

While every abuse is different for each person, how the individuals mind and body functions with such trauma after an incident may also vary. There are many ways that individuals can combat their fears and obsessions and move towards living a more productive life. *There are three things to begin removing (External Victimization Effects.) (1)****You must understand what it is***. External Victimization is what your brain harbors in its memory and your negative speech and behavior is the product of this. Internal Victimization is what you "think" about which fuels the "(external behavior.) (2)* ***Take a "reverse approach"*** *by going back through past events in your mind and work forward to address each issue. (3)****Analyze*** *what led you to the point of the external behavior and work through each individual issue. By doing this, you can back track and re-work your mental state completely.*

The "EVE" Effect
Eliminating Victimization

Being A Victim

Once you understand that you were a "victim" for only "one" day, you will begin to look at the issue differently. When the incident occurred, you became a "victim." The day "after" the perpetrator was long gone, jailed, disappeared, met their maker, or ceased to exist "you" then began "victimizing" yourself over and over again with the memory of what the perpetrator had done.

JUST LET GO!

You did what was natural to do for survival which was to suppress it. Over time, depending on your environment, you began ruminating over it. "Why me," is a constant question. Why was I chosen? Why not someone else? Why didn't I fight back? How could they do this? What were they thinking? Why did I walk home that day, night? Why didn't I close the window, check the locks, carry a weapon, change streets I walked on, leave my purse at home and the list continues...! Then at the next phase, you begin to self-doubt, thinking that "you" somehow were not "worthy" of anything better happening to you in your life. You might think that you somehow brought this on yourself.

You might even think someone else was to blame because they didn't do anything about what they may not have seen, whether they saw it or not. If you believe someone knew what was happening and did nothing, you may want to place a blame there. This becomes the next "trigger" in your mind. Anger sets in towards the person you believe "knew" and didn't "do" anything about the situation to save you, when, like the young girl in the story, her mother had no idea at all. The thing to focus on is that, in reality, the "perpetrator" is the "ONLY" one fully responsible for the acts they committed. No one else! You must first understand that unless there is more than one "clear" perpetrator, then you deal with that "one" perpetrator only. It helps free your mind from going into the vortex of your brains executive center and creating unnecessary havoc!

Now your brain is trying to figure out why you have "Fear" inside you. It is natural to relive an experience we have had whether it is good or bad. However, once you recognize that you are fearful because what happened posed a "danger" to you, your brain begins to give you ways to protect yourself, "NOW!" You may not have been able to do anything more at the time. Your brain doesn't automatically reason that you were only 5 when an incident happened and now are 25. It is giving you things you can do "now" and in the future!

JUST LET GO!

But we take this to mean that we should have done *something "then" which may "not" have been humanly possible! We then ruminate thinking somehow that we didn't fight hard enough or that it was our fault, when it was not!!! We understand that some fear is "good" because it says that you recognize that what happened was wrong and should not be done to anyone. Remember that if you are no longer a child and you "can" do things to prevent this type of abuse from happening to you again, you will do so. If you are an adult and still have "Fear" of the incident from childhood, follow the example of the young woman in the previous scenario helps.* She loved her family and wanted to stop causing them pain by her obsessions with cleaning, stains, darkness, colors of clothing, things being out of line and other behaviors that existed.

She realized that the ordeal was over and had been for some time but she was still reacting to the past "fear" Now she had to learn how to Let Go and "recognize" those reactions to her fears and frustrations and see how they were destroying her future. Writing down all of your "obsessive negative behaviors help you look them in the face. The brain ingests them as you go over the list and read them back to yourself. Ponder them before you begin working backwards through them to dismantle the negative thoughts associated with the incident. Give yourself time to digest why these habits exist.

When you recognize yourself performing the "obsessive habits," jot down what happened "before" the obsession began. Note what the "trigger," **(which is something that takes you mentally back to the time of the abuse) and causes you to use this "obsession" to express your displeasure with what happened in that incident.)** At this point, you will recognize "what" you are "using" to fuel the present "abuse" you are heaping upon yourself by fueling your pain and anger when something in your "current" life goes wrong. The key is to feel better.

Once you recognize why you continue to ruminate over the incident by way of obsessions or withdrawal, you must determine "why" you should let the obsessions or withdrawals go.

JUST LET GO!

You can do this by taking baby steps towards the healing process. If you have a family, focus on them and the love you want to give them instead of the pain that you are holding on to. Remember that the perpetrator is no longer there to harm you because you are able to "protect" yourself. Remember that the abusive act has ceased but what remains is what you must contend with. Do so in a way that will make "YOU" the "Victor!" Give yourself permission to still be "innocent" of the actions that took place since the individuals were the "adults" and had a measure of control over you at that time, but not anymore! They are still the "wrongdoers!" There is one final thing to remember:

> *The perpetrators will pay for what they have done. If you destroy your own life by not living it to the full, you are picking up the perpetrators "debt" of suffering and leaving that as an inheritance to your children. At this point, you want to live for those you love which will in turn help you live for yourself. As a final note....*

Tell Your Brain Positive Things You Want "It" To Believe!

1. I am not to blame for what has happened.
2. I will love myself regardless of what others may feel about me.
3. I will not blame others for what happens to me.
4. I will be aware of any obsessions by writing them down and working through each of them.
5. I am valuable and will not shut myself off from the world.
6. I will seek assistance from those who really care and will help me.
7. I was a "victim" only once and will acclaim "victory" over my acquired obsessions.
8. I will not pick up the "debt" of the wrongdoer by destroying the life they failed to destroy.
9. I will not dwell on the past and destroy my future.
10. I will be a mother, a father, a sister, a brother, an aunt, an uncle, a niece, a nephew, a cousin, a grandparent without fear.

JUST LET GO!

11. I will NOT emulate the perpetrator by violating someone else's rights in order to gain back the perceived power I felt the perpetrator took from me.
12. I AM TAKING BACK MY POWER! I will realize that taking something from someone because someone took something from me only makes me a "perpetrator," Which then would give me no claim for redemption.
13. I will remember that in order to "imprison" someone, you must become a "prisoner." For this reason I take no prisoners.

Remember that you "CAN" overcome obsessive negative behavior relating to abuses you have experienced. Everyone's situation is different. One person's cure may not work for another. But if there has been abuse of any sort in your life, recognize that to undo the feelings you have inherited from this un-warranted action against you, you must take one step at a time and realize that you "CAN" live a better life. It's time to shed the excess baggage of the past and remember that "YOU" have the key to the prison doors you were once placed in... It's up to you to walk out of those doors that were never "Locked!" "OPEN" those doors to your mind and your heart and walk out a "Free spirit!" From this day forward, you will no longer count yourself as a "Victim!"

Just Let GO

JUST LET GO
"PROCRASTINATION"

In everyone's life, procrastination can creep in like a terminal illness. It sneaks up on you like a thief in the night that invades your mind and body. It can block you from making valuable progress in life. Many people have no idea how procrastination begins. It is very subtle and most of us are not aware that it exists until it is almost too late.

JUST LET GO!

What are some areas that procrastination can affect us: Paying bills, personal hygiene, house chores, keeping promises, changing negative behavior, work assignments, getting things done, sticking to projects and being punctual to name a few. When you do realize you are procrastinating by not following through on something, you may go into shock momentarily! Usually there is a strange feeling you get when you realize that you have stopped functioning in a positive manner.

Then you wonder how much damage has been created and begin looking for telltale signs of the destruction. Soon, your focus sharpens and you begin reflecting on bills that haven't been paid on time. You have missed doctor visits. You started to kick smoking, but now are up to two packs a day! Laundry is piling up and your home is a wreck. Nothing is like it once was. What happened? Now you are even skipping the shower? This is serious! You become overwhelmed when you realize you are in "trouble!" Over a period of time of putting things off you now know it is time to put this vehicle in reverse.

You first must stop to consider some important things. If your procrastination is real and you haven't paid attention to your bills, you must consider if you don't pay bills, you may not have a place to live, have food, lights, water, or heat. If you don't do laundry, you will have no clean clothes. If you don' tidy up your home, you have a mess to live in. If you don't shower, you have "NO" friends. We must find ways to break the vicious cycle of procrastination. **First,** start by recognizing that you have a problem. **Second,** Identify what the issue is you must address…make a list. **Third,** take one step at a time to fix each area of concern, but "pair" like issues that affect each other. *Example:* If you have a problem showering, this requires water so when you shower it will prompt you to pay the water bill the same as when doing laundry. The point is, one thing will prompt you to focus on the other. You may begin being aware when taking a shower each day. If you get in the shower and don't have water because you haven't paid your water bill, each time you shower you are reminded to pay the bill.

JUST LET GO!

When you get out of the shower and are "clean," it prompts you to want to put on "clean" clothes. Therefore, pairing hygiene, water bill and Laundry together works well as a prompt. Master these and move on to the next issue. This is a good way not to be overwhelmed and to begin the process! Then you begin again on other areas once you have stopped procrastinating on each area you have worked on. Sometimes doing one thing will fix the others. Over time, you will be doing things on time as needed. Leaving things undone can be critical. At this point…it's time for a "change!" Agree to "Just Let Go" of procrastination. It's time for "CHANGE!" Remove NEGATIVES from your life!"

JUST LET GO OF "INHIBITIONS"

Inhibitions are feelings that cause us to be self-conscious about something and unable to relax or be natural in certain settings. As a child, we may have been shy about doing things in front of others and were inhibited when we were put on the spot.

JUST LET GO!

As we become older, other forms of inhibitions may appear. It may have been that we became anxious around certain people or were unable to feel normal in a specific setting. Inhibitions are not always bad, the same as "fear and anger," is not always bad. It all depends on when these emotions are present with us and how we react to them at that moment. However, some inhibitions are good! When you want to knock someone out cold, our "good" inhibition may stop us from doing so. On the other hand, "negative" inhibitions may prevent us from enjoying ourselves in that same setting with friends or family. As we become adults, many of our childhood inhibitions may soon diminish. However, when they do not, they may manifest themselves later in our lives in strange ways. We may sustain traumatic or negative events in our lives which could cause inhibitions. When this happens, it could very well cause many negative issues that could affect us for the remainder of our adult lives if not reversed. Sometimes incidents happen to us as adults and we are so traumatized that we may become introverted.

We may be able to speak openly, but may inadvertently hide ourselves in other ways. Sometimes people have been known to use food as a way to quiet their inhibitions. They may feel that food helps them by hiding the person that was traumatized. With each pound they gain, they may mentally feel that their long gone predator will somehow no longer see the need to attack them again, so they eat and the pounds continue to pile on. Some may feel that the perpetrator was attracted to them for some reason and if they overeat and is overweight, they somehow will not be a target. However, this is not true. In other instances, there may be subliminal messages from those we love that may leave us with inhibitions we did not know we had until it is almost too late. This next scenario is indicative of an individual who has been handed down negative thoughts and feelings about themselves and over time it has caused them to develop negative emotions and views about themselves. These negative views, though unfounded, created a life altering effect for this person and devastated them. How do people survive the madness of living in a world based on false hope and teachings? Read the account of an individual who was inundated with negative thinking that slipped into her adult life.

JUST LET GO!

THROUGH MY MOTHER'S EYES

*S*ince childhood, a young woman was tormented with the thought of being "overweight." The thought had been forced into her brain by various means as far back as she could remember. Now, as an adult, she tries to live life without self-confidence and a brutally damaged mental state. The reality for this woman is that she has finally recognized that "she" has silently sabotaged her own life and relationship with the man she loved. Over time, she developed many inhibitions which caused her to believe what she was told from childhood. Now that she has lost something very dear to her, there is something that is about to happen to change how she looks at herself going forward.

It has taken a long time for her to come to grips with this reality and she is finally beginning to see the light. Recognizing now, that she focused only on what her mother told her as a child and never delved into the circumstances surrounding the information she received. This negative pattern continued and left her with very little self-worth and her confidence was always low. She did not do well in college because she felt she didn't measure up to her classmates, so she dropped out! From that point forward, everything she did in her life was for the sake of living up to someone else's views and expectations of her.

She thought that this was the only way to be accepted because of feeling that her weight was a disgusting thing. As a child, she had been told that she was fat. Although she didn't feel fat and could do everything other children her age did, she believed every word her mother and other family members uttered to her. They echoed the same negative sentiments. She went through her childhood hearing things such as; "sit down fatty and "come here fatso." She had no other recourse but to obey the commands that were given to her and soon mentally became what they said she was.

JUST LET GO!

She was fed when she wasn't hungry and over fed when she was. Although she was of normal to average weight for her height, and age, she grew up believing she was overweight and ultimately developed an inferiority complex about her appearance. She soon believed she was so unattractive that she wouldn't look at people. She was shy and withdrawn with peers she had known for years. In high school she would shy away from exposing herself even modestly when the girls were required to shower after gym class. Believing they would laugh at her perceived hideous body, she was fearful of rejection. As the years continued into adulthood, she convinced herself that she was overweight and unattractive. In an effort to compensate for the negative mental image of herself, she catered to people around her.

She felt that she had no right to expect anything from anyone because of how she felt about herself. Soon after high school, to her shock, she met a man and though still shy and inhibited, she was told that she should marry this man because no one else would come along to marry someone as "fat" as she was. Fortunately, she fell in love with the man and married him but experienced a horrid realization about her inhibitions from childhood. Being intimate with her spouse became very uncomfortable because of the distorted view of herself and her body. Over time, she refused to dress in front of him...hiding in the closets and would not be caught in any intimate apparel. She was once found sitting in their vehicle during a function where all the guests were at a pool side for brunch. She also refused to accompany her husband on exotic trips for his job.

Though he continued to beg her to go with him, she refused. Her inhibitions were out of control but she did not recognize how bad they were until it was too late. She refused to branch out from this mental drain of inhibitions, believing what had been told to her as a child. The sad result of this issue was that her husband filed for a divorce. The marriage was dissolved abruptly. The woman was devastated but consoled herself by chalking it up to her now, ex-husband leaving her because she was "fat." She cried much of the days and nights.

JUST LET GO!

She was very lonely as a single woman and began "eating" to satisfy her frustrations. She was haunted by her mother's words and finally decided to do something about her negative feelings. She wished for the companionship she once had with her loving husband. The thought plagued her each day as to why her husband had left her so suddenly. One day she was out and happened to see her ex-husband at an outdoor café. Surprisingly he was with a beautiful woman who was twice her size! She was shocked and crushed all at the same time! Confused about her thoughts that her Ex-husband had left her because she was "fat," she decided it was time to find out the truth of why he left her. If it wasn't because she was "fat," then why did he leave? It burned in her heart and she would soon find her answer. She did not dare disturb their seemingly romantic moment, but the next day she decided to call her ex-husband and ask him why he had left her.

When she approached him, it was clear he still had fond feelings for her. When she asked him why he divorced her, what he said shocked her! "I felt you didn't want me!" He said. The woman held the phone as if it were a loaded gun pointed at her head. She wanted to scream, but was further shocked when her ex-husband burst into tears on the phone and poured his heart out. The woman did not know what to say, but realized her eyes were now open. Her ex-husband, was a ships' Captain and travelled six months out to sea. He had begged his wife for years to travel with him to the many exotic ports his ships sailed to. She always refused, thinking she would be laughed at by her husband if she were seen in a bathing suit next to the beautiful girls that lived on these islands where the ships docked. She refused to travel with him. Now, the woman was devastated because of her negative behavior! She hung up the phone and later was moved to tears. Not because of what her ex-husband said, but because she realized there was something else that had caused her mental state other than the thought of being fat! What had prompted her behavior? She would not rest until she found the answer.

JUST LET GO!

She finally realized that she was "not" fat and that the thoughts had stemmed from childhood. She vowed to seek professional help to sort out her feelings of the whys for her horrid mistake she had made in her life due to her inhibitions to let go of negative thinking. She had ruined her life and lost a man that truly loved her. She had relied on what she learned as a child and encased herself in years of unnecessary pain. She spoke with a professional about her childhood experiences and the precepts she had now realized. She shared with the professional how her mother had convinced her that she was fat all of her life. However, she was helped to realize that it was her "mother's" own miserable physical state of being morbidly obese that had inadvertently caused her to teach her daughter that she was fat as a child. It was her mother's sad attempt to deter her daughter from travelling the same path of obesity as she had. The woman soon realized that it was not "her" Image she saw in the mirror, but that of her "mother's.

Soon memories that had been locked away in her mind were reopened. She remembered her mother not wanting people to look at her when she ate. Therefore forcing her daughter to eat in secluded rooms with her. Being forced to eat when she wasn't hungry and sometimes even going without food because her mother had eaten it all. The girls' mother ultimately died from complications of obesity. But, the woman had taken on her mother's mental thoughts as her own. She confessed to the professional that her mother use to cry while stating that she wanted to wear a bathing suit and go to the beach. She loved the water, but was too large to fit in a simple bath tub.

She never went to the beach because she could not leave the house where she resided. The woman's mother died never knowing what those simple things felt like. Worst of all, she had left her young daughter with the chore of carrying her pain and suffering in her own life. She had handed it down to her like an inheritance. Once the professional had concluded her findings to the woman, she left the office and went home to ponder the day's discussion. She vowed that she would change her mindset immediately! It was clear that this had to be done.

JUST LET GO!

She wanted to live life and be happy again. She would "just let go," of her inhibitions, negative feelings, thoughts, images and perceptions she had been saddled with throughout her life. The next day would be a new beginning. Immediately she went out and bought a new bathing suit. A pretty one-piece and a cover up which she felt was age appropriate as her first choice. With her new found courage, she drove to the beach alone to test her feelings of freedom she'd never felt before. She sun bathed for hours for the first time and understood why her mother wanted to go to the beach so desperately. For a moment, she felt as normal as all others on the beach that day. She watched the ships sail out to sea representing her past life that she would never look back on. Vowing to let go of all her negative thoughts and inhibitions, a smile formed on her lips. As she watched the waves go in and out from behind her new sunglasses, her thoughts were no longer interrupted by negative images when thinking of doing positive things for herself.

She had finally given herself permission to "DREAM OUT LOUD." Sipping on her cooler she relaxed for the first time in a long while in the sun. She watched couples playfully chase each other on the beach and marveled at families building sand castles with their children. There was a sense of wellbeing amidst her now and she was no longer bogged down with the inhibitions she once had. When she realized "what" had been causing her to feel the way she did about herself, she was able to clearly address the issues. The beach was beautiful from that day forward. It was a whole new life emerging from a dark place where she use to dwell. Over time, she tossed away all her negative inhibitions and fears about being fat. Her attitude changed and she was able to enjoy life as it was meant to be enjoyed. Soon, she would no longer be alone. She met the man who would later become her second husband on that very beach.

JUST LET GO!

This time, she would be wearing her new "Two piece" bathing suit...without a cover up. She had finally "Let Go," of her inhibitions and started living life to the full. For this woman there was a "bitter, but sweet" ending. She conquered her inhibitions and moved forward with her life in a positive way! Sometimes, recognizing what the problem is can ignite our senses to the solution we need in order to change a negative behavior. It may be that we need to sift through our belief systems. Some of those things we are handed down may no longer "fit" into our lives. When they don't, we may consider revising or discarding them. We don't always have to make a list to start making positive change in our lives but we do need to make an **"EFFORT"** *to "Just Let Go" of things that are no longer beneficial to us.*

JUST LET GO OF THE NEED TO CONTROL

What is control? Why is it necessary or sought after? Control is the power we have to direct things or people. It's a form of lording over or ruling over someone. Control is related to many things and can be seen in different areas of our lives. Sometimes we don't know that we are trying to control something or someone until it's too late. Excess stresses may come from taking on more than we need to which can be due to having or wanting unnecessary "control."

Again, remember that control can be in many forms when it comes to people or things! It could be our spouses, friends, children, work mates, direct reports etc. It could be in-Laws, other relatives, pets, projects and the list can go on forever. We may excuse ourselves for the need for this unnecessary control by saying that we have the "responsibility" to do this or that. But in reality, we "don't!" Don't get this twisted...sometimes you do have responsibilities that may require that you check up on someone in an effort to teach them what they need to know.

JUST LET GO!

But at some point, the person should be required to "get it" and be able to do whatever it is on their own without you. Besides, if you are the boss, then be the "boss!" Anything more than a performance check-up is micromanaging," which is punishable by law in the workforce today. Control can be addictive but you must kick the habit to reduce the extra weight of doing the jobs of more than one person. Namely, your own! If not, you will not be able to "rate" their performance fairly and then you may not be the "Boss" after a short while. It's the same principle when it comes to controlling children. Whether they are ours or someone else's the same principle applies. We must seek ways to allow the child to learn what they need to learn and not use your parental "control" over them to the extent that they are stunted in their mental growth. Many parents make this mistake when their children are young and they control everything.

If they get to the point that they feel "they" the parents are the only one that can do something to their own satisfaction, then at some point the child will stop doing anything at all and not even try! Years will go by and the parents become tired of doing the work of the young adults in their household and now they want to ask the child these questions...
"Can't you do something for yourself?"
"Do I still have to clean your room and take out the garbage for you?"
The simple answer is, "YES." At this point the child has been trained to let "YOU" do all the work at your insistence. All because you wanted to control everything from the beginning. Now the parent is tired and is truly in need of support and trying to let go, but sadly, they have enabled the child in certain areas and they can no longer take charge of those simple things in life. The parent now may have negatively affected their personal health with high blood pressure from working, taking care of the house and the child and realize how their need to control has crippled their own life. It is now a do or die situation. They must allow themselves to begin being okay with not being in control of everything in their life and in those they love!

JUST LET GO!

They now must learn to give their child responsibilities commensurate with what they can handle or the child will never learn responsibility. At this time, it is crucial for the parent to let go of unnecessary control in order to reduce their own stresses! They must stop the madness and realize that everything that needs to get done doesn't require that "They do it!"

Now you can learn to delegate things to others and lighten your load. The only difference between controlling a child and an adult is that the adult is more likely to tell you what is on their mind at some point. If you are controlling a partner in a personal relationship, the word "partner" says it all. They should be able to "help" in any situation that may exist. Some people may be more aggressive than others, but that shouldn't matter. If you control a "partner" in your relationship until they feel as if they are no longer needed, you may soon find yourself minus a partner. Many couples have this problem. When control is out of control in a relationship and the person controlling has done it so long that the controlee stops doing anything but waiting for the controller to do all the work…it gets crazy at some point.

The controller gets fed up one day seeing the controlee doing nothing and now enjoying it. Then the controller wants to tell the controlee that they are not doing enough in the relationship. Well, the controller doesn't realize that over time, they have made their "partner" into a mere "donor." They can chip in when they choose to. They are no longer required to pitch in as a "partner" would do. The controller has now done a disservice to themselves, their children or who or whatever it is they are controlling. So, if you are doing everything in a relationship, beware! In time, you may have major stresses from being overworked. You are taking away any abilities others might have to support the process and you for living a better life. It's time to give up the control mechanism and "share" responsibilities. There will be enough times in life where you may have to carry the load alone. If you still aren't seeing the point of not "controlling" everything.

JUST LET GO!

Think about people who are truly handicapped. Most of them fight to do things for themselves. Why? Because they don't want to burden others to do things they feel they should do for themselves. They try harder to support themselves. Stevie Wonder, a blind musician, plays the piano and entertains people all over the world. He probably earns more than most people that have full sight! Nick Vujicic, a well-known motivational speaker who is a quadriplegic. His positive attitude and motivation inspires others to get up and stop making excuses about their lives and do something about it! He has a successful career. He swims, golfs, boats and does other sports and has a beautiful wife and children. He is amazing! These and other individuals like them who are challenged in some areas but successful, do not hinder others from helping them do the things they "truly" cannot do, but everything else they need done… you'd better get out of their way because they won't need anyone's help! So, when you feel that you must control something around you, remember that the weight you take on at some point will become unbearable. Learn how to "Just Let Go," of the unnecessary control of others and live a fuller longer life!

WHY SHOULD WE LET GO OF NEGATIVITY?

Learning how to identify your negative mind triggers that take you into the "vortex" of life is not an easy task. Especially if you have not planned to go there. You can ruin your entire day in five minutes and six seconds or destroy a romantic evening in less time than it takes to yawn by dredging up "old stuff" that really no longer matters." It's time to "STOP" the madness of holding on to negative thoughts. LOOK at where your life is today and visualize where you want it to be tomorrow. Then, "LISTEN" to your positive inner voice and hear what your mind and heart is saying. Then you can "LEARN" how to "JUST LET GO," of anything negative. This book focuses on the "simple" things you can do to begin letting go of negative mental baggage.

JUST LET GO!

Once you realize that something is too heavy to carry physically or mentally, you can now "Just Let Go!" Once you let it go, "never pick it back up!" Have you ever noticed that in every city on the planet, they have designated "garbage days?" This is a special day that is set aside to take out the "Trash," in people's lives! Letting go of things we don't need is the same as putting the "Trash" out of our lives. Trash is identified as anything that you have gotten the usefulness out of. After something is all used up, you let it go! Also there may be things that we no longer "can" use. When we keep things we can't use anymore, whether it is physical or mental, it is called "clutter."

Clutter is not useful! It's in the way of things that we "could" use if we could see them behind the "clutter." Learn how to let go of your mental "refuse." You can do this by setting aside a certain day and deciding what you no longer need any more in your head and discard it from your mind. For hoarders, you can do the same thing with physical stuff. Start by allotting yourself time to "READ" positive things to replace the negatives you dump out of your head! For some reason, when we remove one negative thought process, we need to replace it with a more "positive" one to add to our memory bank. Remember, what you put into your "memory bank" you will be able to get the same thing out…so, it's time to clean our mental house! Learn what your red flag warning signs are and be able to stop them in their tracks! No longer will you be "close to the edge" with so many negatives that you can't fathom putting another thing in your head even if it is "positive."

When you begin to "ruminate," over the garbage that's in your head, it is time to take the 3 R's approach… **R**egroup, **R**evise and **R**emove any and everything that causes you to become bogged down in life. Take a few moments each week to gander back through the pages of "Just Let Go!" Glean nuggets of life from the many struggles others just like you have conquered. The negative accumulation of thoughts and actions are discarded by using these simple suggestions of letting go of unnecessary "baggage!"

JUST LET GO!

You first remove the negative thoughts, actions and behaviors that clutter your positive decisions in life. Then you Regroup your thoughts and begin putting positive thoughts in place of the negatives. If the thoughts no longer work, Revise them and Remove what is now refuse which creates a complete change in your thinking habits and ability which in turn can change your life from negative to positive!

Always reflect on the fact that "mind hoarding" is a process whereby you hold onto everything in your life good or bad from the time you are born and never let go of anything. Day by day you literally clog you synapse and reroute any positive mental energy you could have to the "hold file" in your brain. If you've ever used a computer, from time to time you have to "empty the trash," from your computer's memory. If not, it will slow your computer down to a turtle's crawl.

To get certain programs to work, you must remove "cookies" from your computer's memory or "brain," which in this instance are not "sweet." Now... that you have a better understanding of what this looks like, take a deep breath....count to three and it's time to take action! The first step is to give yourself permission to Stop, Look, Listen and "JUST LET GO!"

 Just Let GO

JUST LET GO!

The most difficult thing to do in life is to "Let Go"

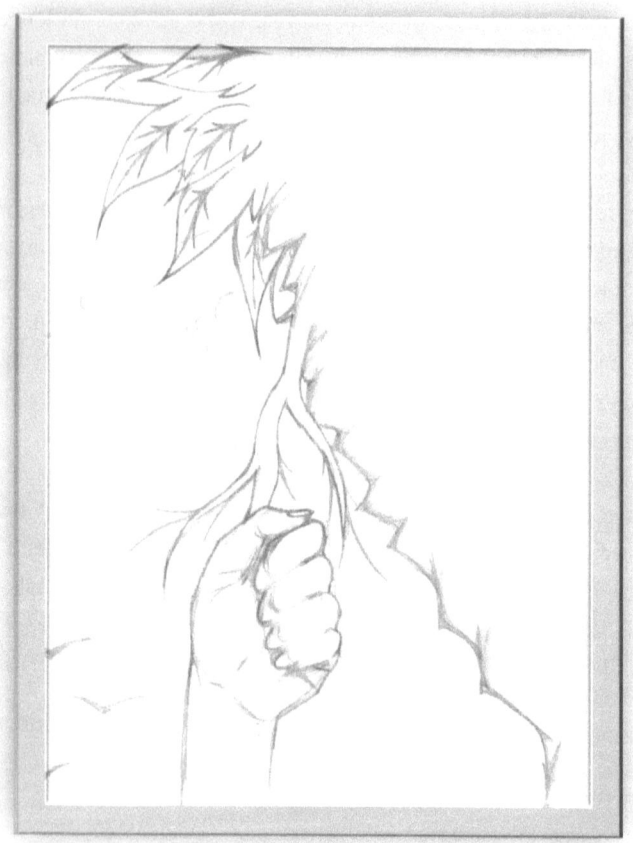

"But it's easier when you already have one foot on solid ground."

JUST LET GO
THE FEAR OF AGING

Aging is a part of everyone's life. It's not natural, but it's part of it. From the cradle to the bone yard, males and females must take that horrifically beautiful journey. How you age has a lot to do with how you treat your mind and body in the process of aging from the beginning. What you eat, drink, and think plays a major role in determining how your body will look and feel in your 20's, 30's, 40's, 60's and beyond. Barring there are no other major health related issues, most people should be able to fare well in the aging process. Many people are fearful of the "O" word because getting "Older" is not what humans want to do. We want to stay young! But for most of us, we'll accept "youthful!" When you think about it, getting "older" is not necessarily as bad as "aging." When we think about someone saying that a person is getting older, that simply means they have lived a year longer than the previous year. However, when they say someone is "aging" that means that the same year they have acquired can be "SEEN" physically on their face or body. That is what we don't want!

Most people don't mind getting older, they simply don't want the signs of getting older to be neck and neck with the "aging" process. But we still must remember that we have no choice in this process except to adjust our thinking where the subject is concerned. Ultimately, it will happen whether we like it or not. We have been eye witnesses to some individuals who fight it tooth and nail trying to deny the inevitable, only to be slapped back into reality when the process shows who really is the boss.

JUST LET GO!

Some may believe that wearing the same size clothing they wore in high school makes them "youthful." Still, it's always good to feel good regardless of what we tell ourselves. The more positive we think, the better we feel! The brain will work with whatever information it receives. That only works from the mental standpoint though. In the instance of getting older, the mind says one thing and the body may say something totally different. You may still be that size 7 but where everything is in that size 7 at 50 is not the same place it was in at 20 years of age. That's okay, we'll take it! It's good to be in shape, or at least in the arena.

Some ask, "why can't we be like the animals?" They don't care about getting old, they just do! A dog readily accepts that they cannot run as fast as they did when they were pups. When you throw them a ball and they are older, they look back at you as if to say, "You've got to be kidding me?" I'm not running for that, you get it!!! And what do silly humans do? They try to run like they were 15 and pass out trying to show the dog what he used to do. Some dogs will even sit down to prove their point. That says that they are using common sense. However, we have witnessed men trying to play basketball and dunk at 50 and 60. Well, that is risky if you are not a professional player and have been conditioned all your life in the professional games.

Dogs don't complain about not being able to bark as loud or run as far when they get older like humans. Men will pretend to be able to hear well into the time when they have completely lost their hearing. You can say something to them like *"honey, look out... a falling rock!!!!!"* After they get out of the hospital, they will pretend they heard you but that blasted rock just found its way to their head anyway. Women may try to wear the see through clothing when a shroud may be more age appropriate for the area they are trying to expose. Understandably, we all want to stay young and supple like a new born baby. Generations are living longer now because of the health trends in our country, but we still are plagued when looking in the mirror at the strangers we have become. Some say... "It is what it is!"

JUST LET GO!

We know it is "not" natural for us to enjoy getting old so we do any and everything we can to slow down the aging process. In fact, common sense tells us, whether we want to or not, the inevitable happens. So why do so many of us waste our time, money and energy trying to halt something that will exist anyway? Let's face it, one day, it seems that you go to sleep as a beautiful young woman or man and the next day, you wake up looking like an older version of each other! That may be a bit exaggerated, but we get the point. For some, that horrible process of "aging" takes a toll on some faster and others scrape by using creams, potions, injections, implants and ~~exorcism~~ I meant, exercise. Most will scrape by but no one gets away clean. Remember, what goes up must come down! Hint, hint…implants.

I'm not knocking it but the process is very subtle and quickly takes a nose dive once aging begins. Granted, many women and men get through the process just fine, but some truly fall through the cracks of life and have a hard row to hoe in the aging process. For those of us who are not aging gracefully, it's always good to have something to fall back on such as a great personality. There are other features we have as we age that may not get hit as hard such as, great hands, nice hair or a beautiful smile or that ever loving swagger. When all else fails, a great personality is the ticket. Soften the blows of aging with the things that you cultivate naturally that should not be affected by age. Start in your youth. These will serve you well later on in life. Even with all of this, the aging process can be detrimental to our mental and physical wellbeing if we put too much time and energy into thinking about it.

Don't get this wrong, women love feeling like women. Firm and supple. Men want to always be muscular and virile in every sense of the word. However for women, these feelings begin at "puberty, menstrual cycles, childbirth, marriage, divorce, menopause, hot flashes, thinning hair, sagging breasts, and that stupid, "turkey neck syndrome!" At some point you begin to feel like, "who cares!" It is what it is! And women don't like what it is! Women do not want any part of their bodies being referenced by any part of a "duck or turkey's" body. That is not fashionable!!!

JUST LET GO!

Call it something else other than a turkey gobble! This is the flesh that appears out of nowhere overnight under the chin after a certain age and just hangs there "like the turkey." Maybe not as bad, but you get the point! Someone truly had a sense of humor. But most of us don't think it's funny when it happens to us. One woman said, "If my skin gets any lower under my neck, just roast me for Thanksgiving!" Her husband of 40 years simply heard the request and agreed to accommodate her.   End of subject!

Still we ask, why? Why do we have to wrinkle and sag??? We just don't seem to be able to win!!! Women are not alone. The fact is that men don't have it any easier, but they seem to adjust better to aging than women do from the visual standpoint. Remember, men think differently than women. They just say less about what is going wrong and ignore when "everything" falls out of place. They will still, shave, shower, put on cologne and tighten their belts and pull their pants up to their necks and once they put their shoes and socks on, they are set for the day!

Someone mentioned that the late Dick Clark had the best skin in the world! He looked almost 35 and amazing before he expired. How did he do it? Well, technology today is amazing and we have our thoughts about it, but most women wish they knew the secret to his youthful appearance. Some might wish to know who his surgeon was because he always looked "great!" But the truth is, many people are able to age gracefully. Aging is not natural for humans, but it is expected. It is also a fact of life like many other things, but it is not natural! For this reason we "naturally" fight it tooth and nail. Don't get it twisted, as men and women age, many things happen to them. For women, some get those little fine whiskers and they might be able to conceal with the use of a lady shaver. However, others may get beards or even an occasional five o'clock shadow! Gray hairs may pop up everywhere hair grows, whether you want it to or not…right!

JUST LET GO!

When it happens, accept it and find a way to embrace it. What about guys and the sagging pecks? If you told a guy he had sagging pecks, he'd probably stone you! Men seem to stay in denial longer than most women. They simple never see that their mid sections have gone to the next level and joined forces with other parts of their body. They sometimes feel that what makes all these wrong things with their body's right, is having someone twice as young on their arms to parade around. You see, for most men, their brains tell them that nothing is wrong with them regardless of what is happening to their bodies or mind. They rarely see the problem of aging in time. They simply tell their brains they need to be surrounded by younger things, more money, faster cars, convertible preferred and they will somehow "blend" in! Like the chameleon.

So being seen at 65 with a 21 year old makes them feel 38. What kind of math is that??? Some call it voodoo economics where nothing adds up. To men…problem solved! All they do is change their "minds" and everything else can stay just like it is. The key is the way you "feel" not the way you look! As women age and date younger men, they call them "Cougars." Why a cougar? Well, a cougar is wily and experienced and in the jungle they go after toothy little rabbits. Easy prey! Well, if you "feel" great, you will exude that feeling in the way you dress, behave, laugh and play in all areas. So sagging cheeks, face and lowered boobs, drooping eyelids, and for heaven's sake, cottage cheesy dimples in our flesh when we put on a couple of pounds? Who knew it would happen? But don't let that stop you from enjoying life as it was meant to be enjoyed!

Regardless of how we feel about it, we all age and some might look better than others but all women and men of all races and walks of life experience many of the same things, they just go through them differently based on their make-up. Still, we shouldn't be fearful of getting older. Remember that with age and grey headedness there is supposed to be "wisdom." As good as that sounds, it doesn't remove the fearful thought that time is ticking us away, one grey hair at a time.

JUST LET GO!

Some individuals may not have many wrinkles and others may resemble the bull dogs with sagging faces even though these pups are ever so cute! Still, no one wants to look like one. But remember, everyone is loved by someone! Some cultures have hairy faces, some more loose skin on the neck and eyes. You can always tell how you will look as you age by looking at your parents. We are all proud to look like our fathers and mothers, but how can we deal with it and not be in fear of getting really old? One thing we can do is remember that from the day we were born, the clock started ticking in the opposite direction. That is why in nine months or earlier, the mother's womb begins to brace itself for removing what it knows can't stay in it any longer than the allotted time frame. You can be born early, but when it gets to that bewitching hour, that baby has to be born one way or another and the clock continues to tick until the bone yard appointment.

Since we all age, the one thing we have in common as humans is that we want to slow down the effects of the aging process. Some people are going to the extremes to appear younger and literally turning themselves into monsters. They are getting what is being called, the vampire, night of the living dead, cheek implants. This is causing a scare in the industry and on the street. The Only thing to be said in this instance is, watch out! Some people do not look good with those implants at all and others may be able to get away with it... But they still get caught later when it all wears off.

You find many that are in the public eye or entertainment industries getting special procedures because they are in the lime light per se. They try to look their best for the world to see. They need to stay young and fresh or many contracts will fall through the cracks. Unfortunately, when the cheeks and other implants began to be affected by the body's natural aging process, those "implants" will be unearthed naturally by the body. Some may forget that on camera, there is much that can be done to "soften" a look, hide a scar and make a person appear fresher by fading the camera lens to Egypt.

JUST LET GO!

However, when you are off camera and in natural light…everything comes back to life and that is when the paparazzi captures the natural photo and plaster it on the National Enquirer for the world to gasp! This is when many go into hiding from the world and try to come back with a blast of plastic everything. No more special appearances or close-ups. There may not be enough muscle tissue to support the extra whatever that's been implanted. The realization is that people are people!!! No one is "ON" 24/7! So when we develop a little skin under the neck, we may choose to have a little nip tuck surgery where the skin is tucked under the chin very neatly.

I know this is supposed to take up the slack of the excess skin in the face where it lacks elasticity, but many may choose to do face exercises to tighten the muscles in the chin and forgo surgery which is unnatural. We talk about many things that we don't like about aging but the best way to age is to get a good start when you are young. Eat right, get plenty of rest, learn how not to worry about everything, avoid being too negative and don't start wearing makeup until you are well into adulthood, this goes for guys too. Save something for later as opposed to doing everything before you begin wearing a training bra.

Our youth today are experiencing way too much too soon! Good rules should be, don't date before you are ready to marry or at least are of age to make an intelligent decision to do so. Waiting will help reduce the stress hormones that cause you to age faster. Letting go of negative, thoughts, feeling, attitudes, and people will help relieve you of bad anger, frustrations and the like. This will help you live a happier life while "smiling" instead of frowning. We all want to pave the way for something better, but we must first find a better way to age. The way we do that is to change the way we "view" aging. Age is not our enemy, "time and gravity is." If you could live forever, who would care how they looked. For humans, we know that as we get "older" our "time" is running out.

JUST LET GO!

We become so desperate to stay "youthful" which denotes that we have more time, but sad to say, even our youths are leaving this life sometimes before their parents due to unnecessary manufactured stresses. Drugs, alcohol, and lifestyle choices. Most of us will do just about anything to halt the process of aging. Many may turn themselves into people our family and loved ones don't even recognize, all for the sake of appearing to look "good," when in all actuality our family and friends will love us regardless!

 **Just Let GO**

Why does it matter what size our lips, hips, bust, or butts are? Oversized tops and extreme bottoms, lips and too much makeup and hair has gone haywire! We recently saw a twelve year old with sculptured eyebrows the same as the runway models! This was true juvenile overkill! Along with the newborn "booties made into pumps on the internet. Our youths are being taught by the adults and the media that this is what "they" should do which is causing them to begin the aging process earlier than they need to. They should be taught to prolong their youth not shorten it! Many children never realize a true "childhood" because they are permitted to do all the things adults do before their minds and bodies can channel through the necessary stages of maturity.

The sensible recommendation is to "STOP NOW BEFORE IT'S TOO LATE!!! Better yet, don't get started! We must "Let Go," of the need to be the most beautiful, perfect person on the outside. Beauty is not our most valuable asset in life. It is actually the "beautiful" person that we are on the "inside" that really counts throughout our lives and not just as we get older.
Virginity is becoming a thing of the past and taking a nose dive in our society! In the long run, people will flock to you because of your kindness and willingness to make yourself and others happy. So, on aging, "Just Let Go" on fighting the aging process and wasting all that precious time which causes us to age.

JUST LET GO!

All for the sake of trying to be someone you can't be again on the outside. Develop that beautiful person over time, "on the inside." Live life to the full. Get a good night's rest, eat healthy meals and exercise regularly. Tell good funny jokes and laugh at anything that is noteworthy to laugh at to include yourself. Never take yourself too seriously. Love hard and play often! If you share your life with those you love they don't care if you have a few wrinkles or not. You'll get so many hugs and kisses from everyone that you won't even notice the beautiful change you have made as life goes on. Your family and true friends will be happy just having you there with them as long as they can. Love covers the rest!

"Think Positive"

JUST LET GO!

THE BRAIN

Humans are born with 1.1 trillion brain cells at birth. Then, we lose 10,000 brain cells each day. By age 80, people lose 4% of their brain mass. The point is, we need to save our brain cells and practice thinking positive every day in order to keep the brain cells active. Remove negative thinking ...doing so can change your life forever!

 **Just Let GO**

"JUST LET GO"

EPILOGUE

In this life, as we have read throughout this book, letting go can be difficult. Over time, we have acquired, learned and inherited bad habits, behaviors, thoughts and perceptions and these can be difficult to shake as well! We have seen how our issues of harboring negative thoughts can stem as far back as childhood, and trauma is a tricky things to shake when you must live through it. But, what we have learned is that anything that is done in life can be "undone." If we tie our shoes, at some point we can choose to untie them when the need arises. If we take a step forward, we can always take a step backwards. Anything we want to change unless it defies the laws of gravity, we can change it. Some things may take a bit more time to undo but it can be done! Taking the 5 simple steps in this book will help re-train your brain in only 7 days! These steps when taken, will help get the ball rolling in the right direction to make the changes we need to make.

JUST LET GO!

If you can agree to "Just Let Go" of only one negative thought, action, behavior or perception each month, in one year you can potentially rid yourself of 12 toxic things that currently clog your brain and sap you of the positive energy you need to live a happier life. Letting go of anything that is negative can make the difference between living a less stressful existence, or combatting chronic depression or disease. It will even lessen fatigue and hypertension. Realizing how tragic toxic thinking can be should make a believer out of you to try anything feasible to rid yourself of this enemy "negativity." Doing so will instantly make your life measurably happier! We understand that some things in life we simply cannot control. Even in those situations there is something positive you can do. (1) Control the things you can and (2) Let the rest go!!!

Don't let life pass you by while holding onto negative thoughts and behaviors you may have inadvertently developed throughout your life. Get rid of negative thinking now while you still can. With the issues of contamination of our air, food and water sources, it is no wonder that our brains are foggy. Undue stress only worsens the problem. Even with all that said, some people will wait until they are unable to make the changes they wish to make in their lives that would have made a difference in how they lived. They will procrastinate and soon may end up in a pickle with the need to create a "Bucket List" to finish out the life they should have lived while they had the chance to enjoy it. Don't let that be you! I urge you to do all the things you want to do "now" that are within your reach while you have the chance and a measure of health to do so. Get rid of all the negative feelings of anger, fear and procrastination. Stop wasting time on things that make no sense at all, like being jealousy or envious of others more successful than you are. Being afraid to secure a life insurance policy because you don't want to think about "IT!" Find ways to think positive and change your outlook on life NOW!

This message should ignite your brain to do the necessary things. There are scores of other areas where you can change a negative to a positive. Just take one day at a time and start living life to the full!

JUST LET GO!

Remember that everything negative we hold on to, drags us further into the grave each day while we yet live. Instead of holding on to negative thoughts, create a positive mental garden where you will plant seeds for positive things to grow in your mind. Learn how to cultivate those positive things each day which will beget other positives along the way. Soon you will have more positives to share with others and then the pollination of your garden will have done a fine work. Thinking positive will reduce wrinkles and negative energy every day because of smiling more! Don't be fearful of growing old. It is actually a privilege to do so. Learn how to get the most out of aging despite the issues we may face while getting there. Work hard at not harboring resentment, anger, holding grudges and being spiteful.

When was the last time you said a kind word to someone you didn't like? Have you mistreated someone who was kind to you? With the world becoming more of a challenge to live in, sow as many positive seeds of love, affection, happiness, patience and kindness as you feasibly can and watch these grow daily. Even in the midst of those weed like attitudes from many people, life still can be enjoyable if we allow it to be. It has been said in a spiritual sense that some of the creator's servants died "Old and satisfied," denoting that they did the things that were pleasing to them and to their maker and while they understood that they were not to live forever at that time, it was okay for them to "Just Let Go," and live life in the way that brought them and others peace and prosperity. Since there is a time for everything, make this your "time" to live your life the best way you can! Let go of anything that you clearly see is holding you back from being the beautiful person you are on the inside to champion a brighter future! The word "live" is an action word. It is time to get moving and be on your job of LIVING! You can do this with positive thinking and remember...

"Your dreams can come true tomorrow, if you let go of negative thinking today!"

~THE BEGINNING~
Not
THE END

Get ready for a new release!
"JUST LET GO FOR TEENS"

JUST LET GO!

The Power of Positive Thinking

Letting go of negative thinking, gives you strength to swim the deepest sea. A positive mind helps protect you from stresses that attack you and me.

Positive thinking is our mainstay, our bread and water that's right, it allows us to soar like an eagle with his wings stretched out in flight.

In this world we need to stay balanced, and keep negativity at bay, we do what is right for all people, and bow down each night as we pray.

So just let go of depression, anger, jealousy and fear. For this old world is passing away quickly, but a positive new one is near.

Order your copy today!

JUST LET GO!

Special Recognition

*Special thanks to my mentor Dr. George R. Monk,
A scholar and champion of positive mind management.*

Quote

"Life is 10% of the experiences we encounter.

The other 90% is of how we react to it."

Brea Nicole
© 2016

www.ingramcontent.com/pod-product-compliance
Lightning Source LLC
Chambersburg PA
CBHW030330080526
44584CB00012B/793